HANUMAN
An Introduction

To the gods
and to the demons
who dance in my dreams

Hanuman holding a branch of the
Sanjivani or "Life-giving" herb;
South Indian bronze talisman

HANUMAN

An Introduction

Devdutt Pattanaik

Vakils, Feffer and Simons Ltd.
Hague Building, 9, Sprott Road, Ballard Estate,
Mumbai 400 001

First printing

Price in India Rs. 295/-

Published by Bimal Mehta
for Vakils, Feffer and Simons Ltd.
Hague Building, 9, Sprott Road, Ballard Estate
Mumbai 400 001. India

Printed by Arun K. Mehta at Vakil & Sons Private Ltd.
Industry Manor, Appasaheb Marathe Marg
Worli, Mumbai 400 025. India

ISBN No.: 81-87111-47-X

Contents

Acknowledgements

This book would not have been possible without:

My parents, who supported me

Yusuf Botawala and Balachandra Ramiah, who helped me get images and information on the Thai Ramayana from Bangkok

Ram Reddy for letting me use the Hanuman clipart in the *Chalisa* pages

Arun Mehta, for believing in the project

The team at Vakil & Sons Pvt. Ltd., especially Mrs. Rajeshree Sabnis (for designing the book and colouring all my illustrations including the one on the cover), Mr. Sudhakar Tawade (for computer layout and graphics) and Mr. Satish Nagvekar and Anil Sahasrabudhe (for editing images on the computer)

Nirmal for searching the web for information on Ramayana and for simply being there for me

To all scholars who have compiled images and translated stories of Hanuman over the years

To Her, my *shakti*, who has enabled me to face every crisis

Thank You.

About this Book

The *Ramayana* is a much-revered Indian epic that contains values most Hindus hold dear. The epic may be seen as bringing to life the eternal struggle between *ritu* and *dharma*.

Ritu is the impersonal and inflexible law of Nature. *Dharma* is the law of society created by man for man that changes with time *(kala)*, location *(desha)* and the personality of people *(guna)*. *Ritu* lets loose the instinct for sex and violence. *Dharma* uses intellect to tame these instincts. *Ritu* gives rise to *matsya nyaya*, the law of the jungle by which might is right and only the fit survive. *Dharma* forces man to live for others, gives rights to the weak and imposes duties on the strong. *Ritu* rotates the cycle of life, causing the sun to rise and set, the moon to wax and wane, the tide to rise and fall, the seasons to change, the plants to wither and bloom, the animals to survive and propagate. *Dharma* domesticates the wilderness to generate a civilized society where man can look beyond survival at the meaning of existence.

Man has a choice: to uphold *dharma* and create a civilized society or to reject *dharma* and live as a beast. The first choice demands overpowering one's instincts and urges and has the potential to transform man into god. The second choice indulges the senses, inflates the ego and makes man a demon.

Both the *vanar*-king Vali and the *rakshasa*-king Ravana are presented as villains in the epic as they succumb to ambition and lust. Both drive their brothers away in order to become kings. Both mock the sanctity of marriage. Both believe in coercion, not compromise. Both are rash, arrogant and self-serving.

By contrast, Rama, the protagonist of the epic, sacrifices everything as he goes about obeying his father, pleasing his subjects and remaining faithful to his wife. His selflessness makes him *maryada purushottama*, the supreme upholder of social values.

Besides Rama stands Hanuman, a handsome, strong and intelligent monkey, who chooses to be celibate and finds fulfillment in selfless service. Though animal, not bound by social law, he achieves what remains elusive to most humans — triumph over the senses and the ego. As a result, he becomes, like Rama, worthy of veneration.

Hanuman is widely worshipped in India for a number of reasons. This book weaves into a single narrative (occasionally taking some artistic liberty for the sake of coherence and simplicity) stories of Hanuman from various sources, such as the original Sanskrit *Valmiki*

Ramayana, Indian vernacular translations as well as Jain, Thai, Balinese, Malay and Vietnamese versions of the epic.

In some of these works, especially the versions from South East Asia, Hanuman is described as having many amorous exploits. In keeping with the Indian tradition that has institutionalized Hanuman's celibacy, I have ignored these stories. But I have included in the narrative some of the female characters who fell in love with Hanuman, including the *apsara* Swayamprabha, the mermaid Svarna-matsya, the sorceress Benjkaya and some of Ravana's wives.

The aim of this book is to help the reader appreciate the many facets of this much-adored monkey-god. It must, however, be kept in mind that this book is only an introduction, not an intensive or an exhaustive look at the monkey-god. It is targeted at the general reader, not the scholar. For those interested in learning more about Hanuman, there is a select bibliography at the end of the book.

I hope this book brings to life the games gods play to amuse and uplift man. May it help readers fathom the mysteries of *santana dharma*, the Eternal Universal Truth. And may it please Hanuman who people believe still lives somewhere in the Himalayas chanting the name of Rama.

— **Devdutt Pattanaik**

Hanuman Jayanti, 2001

Within infinite myths lies the Eternal Truth.
Who sees it all?
Varuna has but a thousand eyes,
Indra has a hundred,
And I, only two.

Five-headed Hanuman; South Indian
painting

The Hanuman Heritage

Chapter I

Sacred Monkeys

Monkeys are considered sacred in India. They are
believed to be the kin of Hanuman, the monkey-god.
To harm a monkey, it is said, brings bad luck.

But there is little reason to venerate or propitiate
monkeys. Unlike cattle, they offer no material benefit.
Unlike serpents, they do not rouse fear. And the devotion
of monkeys is nothing compared to the devotion of dogs.
This makes the origin of monkey-worship in India a bit of
a mystery.

For centuries monkeys in India have been associated with
curiosity, mischief, restlessness, naivety and trouble. This
has given rise to a number of not-so-flattering vernacular
idioms, metaphors and proverbs such as: *bandar nyaya*
(monkey justice) referring to judgement based on extreme
selfishness; *bandar baant* (monkey distribution) meaning
unfair division; *bandar ki topi* (monkey's cap) which is
used when a troublesome person is given another
opportunity to create more trouble; *bandar kya jane adrak ka
svad* (monkeys cannot appreciate the taste of ginger) to
indicate a fool who cannot appreciate quality. Even the
Valmiki Ramayana states that the appearance of a monkey
in a dream is inauspicious.

What then makes the monkey-god Hanuman so popular
in India?

Hanuman, the monkey-god;
Madhubani painting from Bihar

Forest Dwellers

In the *Valmiki Ramayana*, the forest creatures who help
Rama are described as *vanar*s, brave monkeys with the
power to speak, fly and change shape. Jain scholars who
wrote commentaries on the *Ramayana* described *vanar*s not
as monkeys but as sophisticated warriors whose banners
bore the image of monkeys.

Maybe the *vanar*s were forest-dwellers. Some scholars
have traced the word '*vanar*' to the words *vana* (forest)
and *nara* (man). The 'tail' of *vanar*s, they believe, is the
figment of a poet's imagination. They consider Hanuman
to be the monkey-totem of an ancient Central Indian tribe
that befriended North Indian Aryans and fought beside
them against South Indian, non-Aryan, probably
Dravidian, tribes who were deemed *rakshasa*s because they
were opposed to the Vedic culture.

It is possible that the forest-dwellers came to be known as
*kapi*s or monkeys because their way of life (one male
dominating a troop of monkeys with exclusive rights over

Papier-maché mask of Hanuman;
Uttar Pradesh

1

Monkey-warriors; Temple wall carving from South East-Asia (top and bottom)

the foraging territory and the females) reminded the poet of harem-orders seen in monkeys and baboons. Vali's behaviour in the epic parallels that of dominant alpha male monkeys: he acquires leadership by killing or driving away every contender and he asserts his authority by keeping all the women for himself. Sugriva and his followers resemble the band of bachelor monkeys who constantly try to kill the alpha male or infiltrate his harem.

The 16th century Portuguese traveller Nuniz noted that monkeys were worshipped everywhere in the Vijayanagara Empire that extended across much of modern Karnataka and Andhra Pradesh. The people of the land believed that their ancestors were monkeys who became human (civilised?) by the grace of Lord Rama. Today, it is generally accepted that Kishkinda, the land of the monkeys, referred to in the *Ramayana*, is the area around Hampi (Bellary district of Karnataka). The large boulders that cover the land, it is said, were scattered by monkeys as they built the bridge across the sea to Lanka.

Archaic Origins

Some scholars have traced Hanuman-worship to the pre-Vedic cult of guardian-heroes or *vira*s who keep watch over frontiers and keep malevolent spirits at bay.

Images of monkeys have been found in the cities of the Indus valley civilisation that flourished over 4000 years ago. It is not clear whether the images are sacred or secular.

In the *Rig Veda*, the oldest and holiest book of Hinduism, there is reference to a virile and powerful monkey called Vrikshakapi, a friend of the god-king Indra, who many believe was the distant ancestor of the present-day Hanuman.

A Popular Hero

Hanuman made his first appearance in literature in the Sanskrit epics, *Ramayana* and *Mahabharata*, 2000 years ago. Both epics acknowledged his prowess and divinity. As bards travelled across the land, Hanuman's simian feats, superhuman strength, magical powers, as well as his agility and intelligence, amused audiences and won him many admirers. He was the archetypal hero who uses strength and trickery to overpower his opponents.

For the simple folk, he was *sankat-mochan*, the remover of problems such as ill health, baneful astrological influences and sorcery.

The middle ages saw "Jai Bajrang Bali" become the cry of many an impassioned wrestler-warrior who joined the *akhara*s mushrooming on the banks of the Ganga. Hanuman's values of discipline, devotion, strength and

Hanuman carrying the mountain of herbs; Pahari Painting

3

An image of Hanuman installed in Maharashtra to inspire the youth

service were much admired by saints like Samartha Ramadas who saw Hanuman as the perfect divinity under whose grace young men could rally together and rise up against imperial forces.

Cult of Devotion

As the *bhakti* revolution swept across medieval India, Hanuman-worship reached its height. South Indian *Vedanta* scholars like Ramanuja and Madhava identified Hanuman as the perfect manifestation of devotion. The idea that Hanuman was the perfect devotee was also perpetrated in various vernacular translations of the *Ramayana*. The works of the 16th century Hindi poet Tulsidas played a significant role in popularising Hanuman in North India.

In a caste-ridden society like India, the affection of the high-born prince Rama for a lowly but devoted monkey fired the imagination of people.

Five-headed Hanuman trampling a demon; Mysore painting

In due course, Hanuman became one of the few gods in the Hindu pantheon to be worshipped across caste lines by Hindus belonging to different traditions such as the Vaishnavas, Shaivas, Shaktas, Tantrikas and Vedantins. He was, to some extent, even adored by Buddhists and Jains. Over the centuries, the fame of the mighty monkey has spread far and wide, making its presence felt in the arts and the literature of South East Asia as well as the Orient.

Vaishnava Tradition

Vaishnavas are the worshippers of Vishnu, the preserver of cosmic order who incarnates as man or beast to battle the forces of chaos and anarchy. Vaishnavas view Hanuman as the perfect devotee of Rama, Vishnu's sixth incarnation. He helped Rama establish *dharma*, the code of righteous social conduct.

According to Vaishnavas, Rama and Sita revealed the secrets of the cosmos to Hanuman who in turn revealed it to mankind. Hanuman is thus the link between man and divinity. His strength was the result of his devotion to Rama.

In the *Ananda Ramayana*, Hanuman is described as Rama's brother, born of the same sacred drink that made Dasharatha's wives pregnant. The wind-god in the form of a hawk snatched a bit of the drink and dropped it into the mouth of Anjani, a female monkey.

In the Malaysian and Balinese version of the *Ramayana*, Hanuman is described as the son of Rama and Sita. One day, soon after their marriage, Rama and Sita took a bath in an enchanted lake and turned into monkeys. They regained their human forms soon after Sita gave birth to a monkey-child. The divine couple returned to Ayodhya, leaving behind the monkey-child in the care of Anjani and Kesari, a childless monkey couple.

Vishnu riding on Hanuman's shoulders; Temple wall carving from Tamil Nadu

Shaiva Tradition

Shaivas are the worshippers of the world-renouncing Shiva. They view Hanuman as Raudreya, an incarnation of Shiva. Like Shiva, Hanuman displays ascetic tendencies and does not care for fame or fortune.

Shaivas believe that both Shiva and Vishnu descended on earth as Hanuman and Rama to destroy the unrighteous Ravana who had misused the powers Shiva had bestowed upon him. Without Hanuman, Rama was helpless. It was Hanuman who found Sita, built the bridge to Lanka, fought and finally killed Ravana. In his humility, he remained in Rama's shadow and never claimed credit for his feats.

Shiva and Parvati in a lake; Pahari painting

In some texts, Hanuman is described as the son of Shiva and Parvati, born after the divine couple united in the form of monkeys. He was given into the care of Anjani and Kesari, a childless monkey couple.

Shakta Tradition

Shaktas are worshippers of Devi, the mother-goddess who represents the material half of existence. In North India, the image of a monkey is often found along with that of Bhairava at the doorway of Devi temples. The monkey is called *langoor-devata* and is identified with Hanuman. He is considered the doorkeeper of the mother-goddess.

Hanuman won the admiration of the mother-goddess after he helped reunite Sita and Rama. Hanuman treated Sita as his mother and watched over her sons Luva and Kusha. He also killed the sorcerer Mahiravana and offered his blood to the goddess Kali, pleasing her greatly.

Hanuman earned a place in the heart of Devi by never looking upon any woman with eyes of desire or threatening any one with his virility. Hanuman is therefore seen in Shakta tradition as the guardian of women's chastity.

Tantrik Tradition

Tantra forms the occult side of Hinduism. With the aid of chants *(mantras)* and diagrams *(yantras)* the powers of the cosmos are channelled for human advantage.

Hanuman assisting the mother-goddess kill a demon; North Indian miniature

6

Tantrikas invoke Hanuman in his five-headed or eleven-headed form. They believe that Hanuman is the most accomplished of Tantrikas, who has achieved *siddhi*, the eight much-sought-after occult powers: *anima* (ability to reduce his size), *mahima* (ability to increase his size), *laghima* (ability to become weightless), *garima* (ability to increase weight), *prapti* (ability to travel anywhere and acquire anything), *parakamya* (irresistible will power), *vastiva* (mastery over all creatures), *isitva* (become god like with the power to create and destroy).

As Hanuman rescued Rama from Mahiravana, the greatest sorcerer in the universe, Hanuman is viewed as the god who protects people from sorcery and the evil eye. Amulets and charms with the monkey-god's image are therefore very popular amongst Hindus.

Because Hanuman brought the mountain of herbs to save Lakshmana's life, he has also become the patron of the healing science *Ayurveda* and is invoked through *mantra*s and *yantra*s for the removal of various physical ailments such as sore eyes, toothache, snake bite and jaundice.

Hanuman image from Kerala

Tantrik Hanuman with four heads and ten hands; Stone carving from Nepal

Vedanta Tradition

Vedanta forms the mystical side of Hinduism. It considers empirical reality as *maya*, a delusion, resulting from ignorance (*avidya*) born of the ego (*ahankara*). This veil of delusion can be pierced through *bhakti* or devotion to realise the soul or *jiva* within. Devotion helps unite the individual soul (*jiva-atma*) with the soul of the cosmos (*param-atma*).

Vedanta views *Ramayana* as an allegory with Hanuman personifying *bhakti* who unites Sita (*jiva-atma*) with Rama (*param-atma*) after destroying Ravana (*ahankara*).

Hanuman clapping his hands as he sings the praise of Rama; South Indian bronze

Buddhist Hanuman

The Buddha challenged Vedic ritualism and Brahmanical orthodoxy around the 6th century BC and established the Buddhist way of life. As the centuries rolled by, Buddhist monks told people stories of compassion the Buddha exhibited in his previous lives. These stories were known as the *Jataka* tales.

In one of his past lives, the Buddha was Rama who renounced his claim to the throne in favour of his brother when told to do so by his father. He went into exile along with his wife and brother. This story from the *Dasharatha Jataka* makes no mention of Ravana or Hanuman.

In the *Mahakapi Jataka*, the Buddha was the leader of a monkey troop that lived on the banks of the Ganga. To save the monkeys from the wrath of the King of Benares, he stretched himself over the river, grabbed a tree that grew on the opposite bank, ordered his followers to walk over his back and escape to the other side. The monkeys were saved but the monkey-chief died of a broken back. The tale of the monkey who makes a bridge with his own body resurfaces in one version of the *Ramayana* found in Thailand in which Hanuman stretches his tail across the sea and helps Rama and his monkey army cross over to Lanka after Ravana destroys their bridge.

Hanuman using his tail to create a bridge to Lanka; Thai painting

Jain Hanuman

Like Buddhism, Jainism also rose as a challenge to the ritualistic practices of Vedism around the 6th century BC.

Jainism is a monastic order based on non-violence. Jains view Rama as a Baladeva, one of the 63 noble beings who walk the earth during a single cycle of life. In the Jain *Ramayana*, Lakshmana, not Rama, kills Ravana, because Rama is too enlightened a man to stoop to violence.

Jain scholars found the idea that *vanaras* were monkeys ridiculous. They viewed them as warriors who carried flags bearing the symbol of a monkey. They also believed that Hanuman, who helped Lakshmana kill Ravana, had many thousands of wives.

Hanuman image from Cambodia

Hanuman in South East Asia

Tales of Hanuman reached South East Asia through merchant ships sailing from the Eastern coast of India. Hanuman and Rama are popular characters in Cambodian, Vietnamese, Thai, Balinese and Malaysia art and culture even today.

There is, however, one dramatic difference between the Hanuman of India and the Hanuman of South East Asia. The Hanuman in the epics *Ramakirti* and *Ramakien* is not the celibate and modest monkey-god of India. He is a high spirited, reckless, powerful and virile rake who kills demons and charms women.

Some of the women Hanuman charms in South East Asian versions of the *Ramayana* are: Swayamprabha, the nymph who showed Hanuman the way to Lanka; Svarna-matsya, the mermaid who tried to dismantle the bridge to Lanka; Benjkaya, a sorceress in Ravana's court.

Hanuman image from Bali

Mighty Monkey of the Orient

Buddhist monks took the story of the monkey-hero to China where he became extremely popular especially after the Chinese scholar Wu Chengen wrote the novel 'Pilgrimage to the Western Heaven' in the 16th century.

The Hanuman in China is known as the Golden Monkey. He is quite different in character from the monkey-god of India. Though he is strong, agile and intelligent, he is extremely arrogant and audacious. He lives a hedonistic life and terrorises everyone, including the gods, until he is tamed by the Buddha himself.

Golden Monkey joins the monk Huein Tsang on his 14-year journey to India (Western Heaven) and after 81 adventures, helps bring sacred Buddhist manuscripts from the Thunder Monastery to China. In one adventure, the monkey rescues a queen abducted by a monster, a plot quite similar to the one in *Ramayana*. The novel ends

Hanuman image from Thailand

The monkey-hero from China

with both the monk and the monkey entering the celestial pantheon as two new Buddhas.

Accessible Divinity

The monkey-hero in the Orient and in South East Asia never attained the divine status Hanuman acquired in India.

In India, he came to be admired, appreciated and adored for his physical strength, his mental discipline, his wisdom, serenity and humility. He has become the object of veneration for a diverse group of people from wrestlers to scholars, from astrologers to devotees, from Vaishnavas to Shaivas, from Tantrikas to Vedantins.

Hanuman's accessibility has ensured his popularity. While Rama, the august and austere manifestation of the divine, locked within a vast temple complex, seems distant and unapproachable to the lowly devotee, Hanuman — standing at the door, in full view of the public — appears more immediate and eminently approachable.

Hanuman's 'monkeyness' ensures that his awesome power does not intimidate. He is earthy and tangible, not ethereal or transcendent. Through him, the divine comes within reach. Hence, the popular North Indian saying: first Hanuman, then God, *pahle Hanuman, phir Bhagwan.*

Five-headed Hanuman; clay idol
from Uttar Pradesh

Birth of Hanuman

Chapter II

Shiva and Mohini

Shiva, the cosmic sage, once saw the celestial enchantress Mohini dance. Pleased with her performance, he offered her a gift.

"Give me the essence of your spiritual energies," said Mohini. Shiva brought forth the fruit of his *tapas* in the form of a fiery seed. Mohini — an incarnation of Vishnu — took this sacred seed and left it in the care of seven celestial sages, the *sapta rishi*s.

"Guard it well," Vishnu told the sages, "From this will emerge a mighty being called Hanuman. He will help me uphold *dharma*, the law of civilised conduct, when I descend upon earth as prince Rama of Ayodhya."

Shiva with Mohini; Pahari Painting

Vayu and Anjani

At the appointed hour, the seven sages gave Shiva's seed to Vayu, the wind-god, and advised him to give it to a worthy woman.

Vayu was secretly in love with Anjani, wife of the monkey Kesari. He decided to give Shiva's seed to her. He found her seated on a hill worshipping Shiva. He approached her as a gentle breeze. Brushing her lightly, he slipped the celestial seed through her ear into her womb.

Anjani's Past

Anjani was no ordinary monkey. She was once an *apsara*, a celestial nymph who served as the handmaiden of Parvati, the consort of Shiva.

11

One day, frightened of a thunderstorm, she rushed into the arms of Shiva. Displeased by what she saw, Parvati ordered Anjani to leave the mountains and live in the forests as a monkey with Kesari as her mate.

Feeling sorry for Anjani, Shiva declared, "Anjani will bear a mighty son who will embody my spirit."

Birth of Hanuman

So it came to pass, Anjani gave birth to the magnificent monkey-god who became renowned in the three worlds as **Hanuman**.

He was also called **Anjani-suta** after his mother and **Kesari-nandan** after his father.

The wind-god known in the three worlds as Vayu, Pavan and Maruta, was Hanuman's divine father. Hence, Hanuman was named **Vayu-putra, Pavan-putra** and **Maruti**.

He was also **Raudreya**, an incarnation of Shiva, the awesome Rudra.

The gods witnessed the birth of this extraordinary child. His life, they knew, would be an exciting one.

Hanuman with his mother
Anjani-devi; modern illustration

Hanuman's Childhood

Hanuman was a restless child, spirited, energetic and inquisitive, unaware of his own strength. He grew up doted by his parents, bouncing boulders instead of balls, shaking trees instead of rattles.

He was smarter than the *yakshas*, wiser than the *vidyadharas*, more talented than the *kinnaras*, more beautiful than the *gandharvas*, mightier than the *devas*, braver than the *asuras*.

The celestial spirits, though in awe of Hanuman's powers, were disturbed by his impetuousness. They feared his innocent pranks could lead to cosmic confusion.

Hanuman trying to catch Surya, the sun-god; modern painting

Havoc in the Skies

One day, Hanuman saw the rising sun. Mistaking it to be an orange coloured fruit, he rushed towards the horizon and tried to grab the solar disc.

It was the time of the solar eclipse and the dragon Rahu was on his way to darken the sun. Hanuman looked at the dragon, mistook it for a worm and tried to catch it.

Fearing the worst, the sun-god Surya and the dragon Rahu sought the aid of Indra, lord of the skies. Indra mounted the cloud-elephant, Airavata, picked up his weapon, the dreaded thunderbolt known as *vajra*, and rushed to the sun-god's defence.

The clouds rumbled, and lightening flashed across the darkened skies. But neither Indra nor his mount could scare Hanuman away. They only fuelled his excitement. Thinking Airavata to be a toy, Hanuman grabbed its trunk and leapt on its back.

Irritated by the child's spirited nature, Indra struck Hanuman with his thunderbolt. Wounded, Hanuman fell from the skies, hurtling violently towards the ground.

Vayu's Wrath

Vayu rushed to Hanuman's rescue and caught him in mid-air. The sight of his mighty son, lying helplessly in his arms with a broken jaw, infuriated the wind-god. He sucked away all the air from the cosmos. "Let those who harmed Anjani's son choke to death," he said angrily.

There was panic in the cosmos. Without air, life in every plane of existence was threatened. "Please forgive our rash behaviour, noble Vayu," said the breathless gods. "To make amends we grant your son powers that will make him greater than the gods."

13

Hanuman is Blessed

The *deva*s said, "His body will be as strong as thunder, his mind will be as sharp as lightening. Fire will not harm him, temptations will not distract him. He will therefore be known as **Vajranga-bali**."

The *asura*s said, "He will have the power to change the size and shape of his body at will."

The planets, *graha*s, said, "He will have power over all the celestial bodies. He will be able to restrain even the baneful influences of Mars, *Mangal*, and Saturn, *Shani*."

Brahma, father of the cosmos, said, "He will live longer than any creature in the cosmos."

Pleased with these boons, Vayu released air back into the cosmos. Hanuman regained his consciousness and returned to his parents, sobered by this experience.

The cosmos heaved a sigh of relief.

Gods blessing Hanuman and his parents Kesari and Anjani; illustration by author

14

Hanuman Befriends Sugriva

Chapter III

Hanuman's Education

Hanuman decided to educate himself and chose
Surya as his guru. "You see everything there is to see in
the universe and you know everything there is to know.
Please accept me as your pupil," he requested the
sun-god.

Surya hesitated. "I don't have the time," he said. "During
the day I ride across the sky; at night I am too tired to do
anything."

"Then teach me as you ride across the sky during the
day. I will fly in front of your chariot, facing you from
dawn to dusk."

Impressed by Hanuman's clever plan and his
determination, the sun-god accepted him as his pupil.
Hanuman flew before the solar chariot withstanding the
glare until he became well versed with the four books of
knowledge called the *Veda*s, the six philosophies or
*Darshana*s, the sixty-four arts or *Kala*s, the one hundred
and eight occult mysteries of the *Tantra*s.

Surya, the sun-god; stone sculpture
from Orissa

Hanuman Pays his Fees

In time, Hanuman became a master of literature,
grammar, politics, commerce, economics, music, the arts,
the sciences, philosophy, even mysticism and the occult.

After completing his education, it was time to pay
his fee.

Surya, the sun-god, educating
Hanuman; illustration by author

15

Sugriva, the monkey-son of Surya;
South Indian wood carving

"Watching you study was payment enough," said Surya. When Hanuman insisted that he wished to give something to express his gratitude, the sun-god said, "Please look after the welfare of my son Sugriva."

"So be it," said Hanuman and made his way to Kishkinda, the land of the monkeys.

Sugriva and Vali

Kishkinda was a dense forest, rich in fruit trees, that was inhabited by *vanar*s, monkeys with the power of flight and speech. Like the *yaksha*s and the *rakshasa*s, the *vanar*s were descendants of sage Pulatsya, one of the seven celestial sages.

Riksha was the leader of the monkeys who lived in Kishkinda. He once fell into an enchanted pool and turned into a woman. Both, the sky-god Indra and the sun-god Surya fell in love with the female Riksha and she bore each of them a son. Indra's son was her first-born Vali. Sugriva was her second child, the son of Surya. After bearing the sons, Riksha regained his male form.

When Riksha died, in keeping with the law of the jungle, the monkeys fought each other for the position of leader. Vali successfully killed or maimed every other contender to the throne and assumed leadership of the monkey troop. He declared himself sole lord of all the trees and all the female monkeys in Kishkinda.

16   Indra and Surya enchanted by the female Riksha; Mughal painting

Monkeys cheering Vali at his coronation; Chitrakathi painting from Maharashtra

As the dominant male Vali was not obliged to share anything with anyone. But he shared everything with Sugriva, his younger brother, whom he loved very much. Sugriva loved Vali too and served him dutifully.

In time, Vali selected the extremely beautiful and extremely intelligent Tàra to be his mate. She bore him a son called Angada.

Sugriva chose Ruma as his mate.

Life in Kishkinda was good.

Vali Tries to Kill Hanuman

When Vali became lord of Kishkinda, Hanuman was still in his mother's womb.

Once, a sage told Vali that Anjana, wife of Kesari, was pregnant with a child who would grow up to be a mighty monkey. The information made Vali insecure. "In time Kesari's son will have the strength to overthrow me. I must kill this contender before his birth."

Vali created a missile using five metals: gold, silver, copper, iron and tin. When Anjana was asleep he pushed the missile into her womb. An ordinary child would have succumbed to this dastardly attack. But not Hanuman. He was manifestation of Shiva's spiritual energies, born of the lord's fiery seed.

When Vali's missile touched Hanuman's body it melted and turned into earrings. Hanuman was born wearing these earrings. They were trophies of his first battle, fought while he was still in the womb.

Tryst with Dhundhubi

One day, a *rakshasa* called Dhundhubi came to Kishkinda and began harassing the monkeys. He ate their fruits and molested their women.

17

Enraged, Vali bared his teeth, beat his chest and declared his intention to kill the intruder. Fearing for his life, Dhundhubi hid in a cave. Vali pursued him inside and challenged him to a fight.

Hours passed. Sugriva, who was waiting outside the cave, could hear the sounds of battle: rocks being hurled, blows being exchanged.

Hours turned into days. The battle continued.

Then Sugriva heard a bloodcurdling cry, followed by complete silence. The fight had ended. Someone had won. But who?

As he did not hear Vali's triumphant yell, Sugriva presumed that Dhundhubi had killed his brother. So he rolled a huge boulder and sealed the mouth of the cave, hoping to trap his brother's killer forever.

Like Sugriva, the monkeys of Kishkinda also concluded that the wretched *rakshasa* had killed their leader. In keeping with the law of the jungle, Sugriva, who was the second in strength, assumed leadership of the troop.

Sugriva waits outside the cave where Vali is busy fighting Dhundhubi; Pahari painting

Vali's Rage

But Vali was not dead.

Vali kills Dhundhubi; Rajasthani painting

After killing the demon he had been simply too exhausted to rush out of the cave or shout in triumph. When he recovered his strength, he was very surprised to see

Vali finds Sugriva on his throne; Chatrakathi painting from Maharashtra

the boulder at the mouth of the cave. He pushed it aside with great difficulty and returned to his kingdom expecting a great welcome. Instead, he found Sugriva sitting on his throne. Blind with rage, he accused Sugriva of treachery.

"But I thought you were dead," explained Sugriva.

"You didn't even wait long enough to be sure; you were too much in a hurry to be king."

Escape to Mount Rishyamukha

In his fury, Vali chased Sugriva out of Kishkinda, giving him not even a chance to clear his name. "I will follow you till the ends of the earth and break your neck," Vali swore.

Vali pursued Sugriva relentlessly until Sugriva sought refuge in the hermitage of sage Matanga that stood on the slopes of Mount Rishyamukha, very close to the river Pampa.

This was one place, Sugriva knew, Vali would not dare enter.

Long ago, Vali had killed a wild buffalo that was running amuck in Kishkinda and hurled its carcass into Matanga's ashram. The sage was so angry that he had cursed Vali, "If you ever come near my hermitage your head will burst into a thousand pieces."

Sage Matanga curses Vali for hurling the buffalo's carcass into his hermitage; Rajasthani painting

19

Hanuman catches Vali's feet as he tries to kick Sugriva; illustration by author

Sugriva's Humiliation

Vali did not enter Matanga's hermitage. Sugriva felt safe but trapped, for if he ever stepped out, he knew Vali would kill him.

Meanwhile, frustrated by is inability to catch Sugriva, Vali vented his rage on Sugriva's family. He killed his brother's children and forced his mate Ruma to become part of his harem.

But the anger and sense of betrayal remained.

To vex Sugriva, Vali would each day climb the hill opposite Mount Rishyamukha and terrorise his brother with abuses, threats and displays of strength. He would holler and scream, beat his chest, gnash his teeth, hurl boulders and trees, and shout, "Sugriva, you coward, you traitor, I have killed your children and claimed your wife as my own. Kishkinda has forgotten you; you are as good as dead."

Sometimes, to provoke Sugriva still further and to force him out of his mountain refuge, Vali would fly over Mount Rishyamukha and, without stepping on the hill, kick Sugriva on the head.

It was in these unhappy circumstances that Hanuman met Sugriva.

Hanuman Defends Sugriva

"Every day I am terrorised by Vali; every night I am tortured by visions of his vengeance," Sugriva told Hanuman.

Hanuman felt sorry for Sugriva. The next time Vali tried to kick Sugriva, as he flew over the hill, Hanuman caught hold of his feet.

Vali recognised the son of Kesari. "If this monkey manages to drag me down to the hill of Matanga my head will burst into a thousand pieces."

To escape, Vali moved upwards but Hanuman dragged him downwards. The two were of equal strength and so neither succeeded in pulling the other towards him. To end the stalemate, Vali struck a deal. "I will stop tormenting Sugriva, but he will not be allowed to return to Kishkinda as long as I am king."

"So long as you promise not to harm Sugriva, I promise never to fight you," said Hanuman. Vali agreed and Hanuman let him go.

Hanuman's promise pleased Vali. He was relieved to learn that the son of Kesari, unlike Sugriva, was not a contender to his throne.

Hanuman raising his hand to punish
the wicked; a shrine in Karnataka

Haven of Rebels

Reconciled to a life in exile, Sugriva made Mount Rishyamukha his home. He never left the hill, too frightened of Vali to venture out. He relied on Hanuman to bring him news of the outside world.

In time, Sugriva was joined by many more monkeys, all those who were discontented with Vali's rule. Mount Rishyamukha became a haven for rebels. "Vali is a tyrant. He has kept all the women and the best of trees for himself. Good leaders always share their wealth with their subjects," they complained.

"If I were king, I would share all I had with you," said Sugriva. The rebel monkeys cheered and rallied around him. He became their leader. All were united by their hatred for Vali.

Monkeys unhappy with Vali's rule join Sugriva; Andhra painting

Hanuman Meets Rama

Chapter IV

The Flying Chariot

One day, Sugriva and Hanuman saw a chariot flying over Mount Rishyamukha moving in the southerly direction. They could hear a woman's cry and a man's laugh.

They noticed that the woman in the aerial chariot was casting off her ornaments as if to mark a trail.
They picked up the ornaments from the forest floor and found them to be exquisite: precious gems studded on delicate leaves of gold. It could only belong to a princess. Who was she?

It was a mystery that Hanuman was determined to solve.

Monkeys atop Rishyamukha see Ravana taking Sita to Lanka; Andhra painting

Strangers in the Forest

A few days later, Hanuman saw two strangers on the banks of the river Pampa. They were young men: one dark, one fair. There was a regal air about them. But they were dressed like hermits: clothes of bark, matted hair. They carried weapons: bows, arrows, swords, axes and spears. Both looked sad, as if a great calamity had descended upon them. The dark youth had tears in his eyes, an unsteady gait, and looked especially miserable. Who were they?

"I think they are Vali's spies, sent here to kill me," said Sugriva.

Before jumping to conclusions, Hanuman decided to investigate. Using his powers he disguised himself as a sage. Rosary in his hand, with sacred marks on his head, he approached the two youths.

23

Hanuman introducing himself to Rama and Lakshmana; Pahari painting

Hanuman Meets Rama

"Greetings strangers!" said Hanuman, "What brings you to this desolate spot." The strangers stopped on their tracks and looked at him warily. They reached for their swords. "I am sorry if I startled you. I am a hermit. I live in this forest and in the years I have been here, you are the first human being that I have come across."

Turning to the fair youth, the dark stranger whispered, "I don't think this man is a demon. Look at the way he looks, the way he talks. His language is chaste, his diction is clear, his mannerisms civilised. He must be the holy man he claims to be." Then, turning to Hanuman, he said, "Forgive our suspicions. Events in the recent past have made us wary of everything in this forest. Let me introduce myself. I am Rama, prince of Ayodhya, eldest son of the late Dasharatha. This is my younger brother, Lakshmana."

Hanuman Sheds his Disguise

Hanuman was relieved to know that neither youth was associated with Vali. But there were questions: What were they doing in the Kishkinda? Ayodhya was way up north in Aryavarta, beyond the jungles of Dandaka and the hills of Vindhya. And what events had made these young men so nervous? Hanuman decided to ask questions later. First he had to shed his disguise.

When Hanuman revealed his true form, Lakshmana pulled out his sword fearing that he was a demon.

Hanuman pacified Lakshmana, introduced himself and invited the two brothers to Sugriva's abode. As they looked too tired to climb the hill, he increased his size, picked them up, placed them on his shoulders and flew to Mount Rishyamukha.

On the way, he told them all about Sugriva and his estrangement with Vali.

Sons of Dasharatha

After they had eaten and rested, Rama and Lakshmana told Sugriva about themselves:

King Dasharatha of Ayodhya, scion of the Raghava dynasty, ruler of Kosala, had three wives — Kausalya, Kaikeyi and Sumitra — but no children. So he invited sage Rishyashringa to perform a *yagna* and propitiate the gods. The gods appeared with a pot filled with a divine fluid that would make Dasharatha's queens pregnant.

Dasharatha divided the divine fluid between his chief queen Kausalya and his favourite Kaikeyi. The two queens, in turn, gave a share to Sumitra. As a result, the three queens gave birth to four sons: Rama by Kausalya, Bharata by Kaikeyi, Lakshmana and Shatrughna by Sumitra. Rama and Lakshmana were inseparable, as were Bharata and Shatrughna. The four princes were educated by sage Vasistha.

Rama and Lakshmana on Hanuman's shoulders; Kondapalli doll from Andhra Pradesh

Birth of Rama, Lakshmana, Bharata, Shatrughna; Pahari painting

The marriage of Rama, Lakshmana,
Bharata and Shatrughna;
Andhra painting

The August Prince of Ayodhya

Right from the start, Rama's mild and gentle disposition caught the eye of the people of Ayodhya. He was stoic and serene, noble and upright, august and mature, winning the admiration and veneration of all those who met him.

Such was the purity of Rama's being that the touch of his foot liberated sage Gautama's wife Ahalya from a curse: she had been turned to stone by her husband when he discovered her being unfaithful in the arms of Indra, king of the gods.

When Rama learnt that *rakshasa*s were contaminating sage Vishvamitra's sacrificial altar with blood and bones and preventing him from performing his *yagna*, he rose to the sage's defence, picked up his bow, went to the forest, and kept the trouble-making barbarians at bay.

In gratitude, Vishvamitra took Rama to Mithila, capital of Videha, and showed him the divine bow of Shiva that was in King Janaka's possession.

Rama breaking the divine bow of Shiva to win Sita's hand in marriage; Pahari painting

Rama Marries Sita

"No living creature, other than Janaka's daughter Sita, has the strength to pick this bow. Sita is no ordinary girl; she was born out of the earth, ploughed out of the sacred fields of the mother-goddess. Janaka has declared that the man who will string Shiva's bow will win Sita's hand in marriage," said Vishvamitra.

Encouraged by the sage, Rama bent down, picked up the bow and bent it so hard that it broke. The sound of the breaking bow shook the earth. Impressed, King Janaka embraced Rama and let him marry Sita.

Janaka's three nieces Urmila, Mandavi and Shutakirti were given in marriage to Rama's three brothers Lakshmana, Bharata and Shatrughna.

Rama Exiled

Soon after Rama's marriage, Dasharatha decided to renounce his throne, crown Rama king and retire to the forest. However, on the eve of the coronation, Kaikeyi demanded the two boons he had promised her years ago, the day she had saved his life in battle by using her arm to replace the broken axle of the war chariot. "I want Rama to live in the forest as a hermit for fourteen years and I want my son Bharata to be crowned in his place."

On hearing this, Rama — without remorse or resentment — abandoned his royal robes, wore clothes of bark and set out for the forest. Sita, his dutiful wife, followed him. So did his brother Lakshmana. The people protested,

Rama, Lakshmana and Sita set out
for the forest while the people of
Ayodhya mourn; Pahari painting

but Rama refused to question his father's decision. "For a
civilised society to function, a husband must keep his
promise to his wife and a son must obey his father.
Otherwise there will be anarchy." So saying Rama left
the city of Ayodhya. Soon after, Dasharatha died of a
broken heart.

When Bharata was given the crown of Ayodhya he
renounced it immediately and chose to live like a hermit
in the village of Nandigrama outside Ayodhya. He placed
Rama's sandals on the throne and served as regent until
Rama returned.

Sita's Bridal Finery

Like her husband, Sita also wished to abandon her royal
robes and ornaments and wear clothes of bark. But she
was stopped by the royal women who said that it was
inauspicious for the husband if the wife removes her
bridal finery.

Rama, Lakshmana and Sita with sage
Atri and his wife Anasuya;
Pahari painting

In the forest, Sita met Anasuya, the wife of sage Atri, who not only spoke of the sacred value of a woman's apparel but also gave Sita a magical sari that would never get soiled or spoilt despite years of use.

Life in the Forest

For thirteen years, Rama, Lakshmana and Sita moved south, away from Ayodhya. They made their way out of the fertile land of seven rivers known as Aryavarta, over the Vindhya mountains, through the Dandaka forests, into the southern part of Jambudvipa, the rose-apple continent of India.

The forest was no sylvan retreat — fire, rain, anywhere, anytime. There were thorny bushes and poisonous fruits. There were days without food and nights spent fighting off insects, reptiles and hungry predators.

Being a hermit, Rama could not even take solace in conjugal company.

Occasionally, the trio found relief in the company of sages. Often, they had to contend with hostile tribes. Sometimes they sought shelter in caves; at other times in straw huts. They would camp for a few days beside a river or a lake and then move on. For that is what hermits do.

Tryst with Surpankha

Once, when they were camping in Panchavati on the banks of Godavari, a *rakshasi* called Surpanakha approached the brothers. Introducing herself as the sister of Ravana, king of the *rakshasas* and lord of Lanka, she sought their amorous embrace. Rama refused because he had a wife already. Lakshmana refused because he was too busy serving his brother.

Surpanakha approaches Rama; Kutch wall painting

29

Rama shooting down the golden antelope that turns out to be a demon in disguise; Chitrakathi painting from Maharashtra

Piqued by the rejection and holding Sita responsible for the failure of her charms, Surpanaka attacked Sita. Lakshmana pulled her away and to teach her a lesson chopped off her ears and nose. To avenge this humiliation, Surpanaka returned with two fierce *rakshasa*s Khara and Dushasana. Rama picked up his bow and drove them away.

The Golden Antelope

A few days later, Sita saw a golden antelope and begged Rama to catch it for her. Rama set out armed with a bow but did not return for hours. Anxious, Sita forced Lakshmana to go in search of her husband.

The deer turned out to be shape-shifting *rakshasa*. Rama and Lakshmana realised this was an elaborate ploy to lure them away from the hermitage. When they rushed back, they found no trace of Sita. They looked around and came upon a vulture called Jatayu whose wings had been cut and who was bleeding to death. Before breathing his last, Jatayu whispered in Rama's ears, "My wings were cut when I tried to stop Ravana, the ten-headed king of the *rakshasa*s, from carrying Sita away in his flying chariot. He was heading south."

With that lead, Rama and Lakshmana began moving south looking for Ravana's whereabouts. That is what brought them to Kishkinda.

Sita's Jewels

The tale of Rama's selfless renunciation of his crown moved Hanuman. He realised Rama was no ordinary man, but a being worthy of veneration.

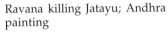

Ravana killing Jatayu; Andhra painting

Sugriva proceeded to tell Rama about the chariot carrying a man and a woman that he had seen flying over Rishyamukha a few days earlier. Hanuman brought out the ornaments the monkeys had collected from the forest floor. Both Rama and Lakshmana identified the ornaments as those belonging to Sita and lamented her plight.

Rama asked Sugriva if he knew where Ravana lived.

"Lanka is located somewhere in the south," replied Sugriva. "No one really knows where."

Birth of Ravana

Sugriva told Rama all he knew about Ravana:

Long ago, Shiva gave a discourse on the Vedas and the Tantras atop mount Kailasa. All the sages moved to the North to hear him speak. As a result, there was no holy man in the south. To correct the imbalance, Shiva ordered the sage Agastya to move south. Agastya crossed the great plains of Aryavarta, the Vindhya mountains and the Danaka forest and made his way to the southern half of Jambudvipa.

One of the sages who accompanied Agastya was Vaishrava, the grandson of Brahma himself and son of Pulatsya, one of the seven celesial sages. Vaishrava had two wives. One was a *yakshi* who gave birth to Kubera and the other was a *rakshasi* who gave birth to Ravana.

Ravana Drives Away Kubera

With Shiva's blessings, and with the aid of the celestial architect Vishwakarma, Kubera built a golden city called Lanka somewhere in the south.

Jealous of his brother's prosperity, Ravana performed austerities to win Shiva's favour. He designed a lute, using one of his ten heads as the gourd, his arm as the beam and his nerves as the strings. He called this lute the *Rudra-vina* and dedicated it to Shiva. He also composed the *Rudra-stotra* hymn in Shiva's honour. Pleased, Shiva gave Ravana the Chandrahasa sword. Wielding this sword Ravana swooped down upon Kubera's city, drove his brother out and crowned himself king of Lanka.

Kubera then moved north and sought refuge on Mount Kailasa where he built the radiant city called Alaka. Shiva warned Ravana never to attack Alaka. "Otherwise your head will burst into a thousand pieces."

Ravana had claimed Kubera's aerial chariot, the *Pushpaka Vimana*, when he conquered Lanka. Riding this flying chariot, wielding his divine sword, Ravana indulged in an orgy of rape and plunder.

Sita throwing her jewels towards monkeys; Pahari painting

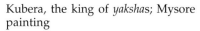

Kubera, the king of *yakshas*; Mysore painting

31

Ravana and the Monkeys

Ravana once kicked a hermit and called him a monkey. Enraged, the hermit cursed Ravana that monkeys would be the cause of his downfall.

Some time later, Ravana came upon the monkey-king Vali meditating on the banks of the Pampa. He decided to tie Vali's tail to the wheel of his chariot just for fun.

Divining Ravana's intention, Vali lengthened his tail, wound it around Ravana, kept him bound for days, dragging him all over Kishkinda like a dog on a leash, until Ravana apologised and promised never to enter Kishkinda or trouble any monkey.

Vali captures Ravana with his tail

Ways of the Forest

Sugriva told Rama that Surpanaka was indeed Ravana's sister and that Ravana, in his quest for power, had accidentally killed Surpanaka's husband. To make amends, he had given his sister rights over all the forests in southern half of Jambudvipa.

Hanuman explained that Surpanaka used force to have her way with Rama as any forest creature would because in the jungle might was right.

Rama said, "The law of the jungle is for animals only, not for creatures capable to discipline and discrimination. In the wilderness there is no compassion. Only the fit survive. In a civilised society, however, animal instincts need to be bridled so that the weak have rights too. *Dharma* is the law of civilisation based on duty, not desire, that ensures social stability. He who upholds *dharma* is an *arya*; he who does not is a *rakshasa*."

Hanuman saw the wisdom in Rama's words. "What will you call Vali, Sugriva's brother, then? He drove Sugriva out of Kishkinda and claimed Sugriva's wife Ruma for himself."

"An animal, a barbarian — no different from Ravana. Both believe in *matsya nyaya* — the right of the strong to dominate the weak. Both have become kings by force. Both do not respect the sanctity of marriage. If civilisation needs to be established, the likes of Vali and Ravana, need to be destroyed."

Rama's Prowess

"You talk big, but how do we know you have the strength to stand up to Vali and Ravana?" asked Sugriva.

In response, Rama decided to demonstrate his strength and skill.

Ravana, king of *rakshasas*; North Indian miniature

First, he found the carcass of the buffalo that Vali had kicked into Matanga's hermitage. Rama kicked it out with such force that it disappeared beyond the horizon.

Rama then picked up his bow and shot an arrow that pierced through seven palm trees and a rock before turning around like a boomerang and returning to his quiver.

After this display of strength and skill, Sugriva realised he had found a strong ally and friend in Rama. Hanuman was convinced that this prince of Ayodhya, belonging to the Raghava dynasty, was no ordinary mortal — he was Vishnu incarnate.

Rama shooting an arrow through seven palm trees; Pahari painting

Sugriva Challenges Vali

Hanuman brokered a deal between Sugriva and Rama. Rama would help Sugriva overthrow Vali and Sugriva would help Rama rescue Sita. Together they would bring civilisation to the wilderness of the south.

Instructed by Rama, Sugriva went to Kishkinda and challenged Vali to a fight. Rama, meanwhile, hid in the bushes, waiting for a opportune moment to shoot his arrow and kill Vali. Unfortunately, when Vali and Sugriva started to fight, Rama could not distinguish between the two brothers; they looked so alike.

Vali disregards his wife Tara's advice and accepts Sugriva's challenge to a fight; Pahari painting

Rama shoots an arrow at Vali as he fights Sugriva; painting from Bali, Indonesia

Vali gave Sugriva a sound thrashing and would have killed him had he not rushed back to the slopes of Rishyamukha.

Death of Vali

When Rama explained why he had failed to shoot Vali down, Hanuman suggested, "Sugriva should challenge Vali again. Only this time he should wear a garland of forest flowers round his neck so that he can be distinguished from his brother."

Sugriva did as he was told and Rama did not find it difficult to shoot an arrow straight through Vali's heart.

As Vali lay dying, he accused Rama of being unfair. Rama said, "He who lives by force cannot demand fairness in death. The rule of civilised warfare applies only to upholders of *dharma*. You understand only the language of the jungle and that is precisely the language my arrow has spoken."

Sugriva's Coronation

By the law of the jungle, after Vali's death, his killer would automatically become king with the right to kill Vali's children and the right to claim Vali's wives.

However, determined to make *vanar*s adopt the law of civilisation, Sugriva broke with tradition. He asked the monkeys of Kishkinda if they wanted him as their king. When they agreed, he asked Rama to crown him in the

Hanuman at Rama's feet;
Tanjore painting

Lakshmana anoints Sugriva, lord of monkeys; Mysore painting

ritually prescribed manner. The Vedic ritual, Sugriva knew, that would make him the supreme upholder of *dharma* in the eyes of the gods. He would be held responsible for instituting and maintaining the law of civilisation in Kishkinda.

Sugriva then asked Tara, Vali's beautiful and intelligent wife, if she was willing to be his queen. She agreed. Finally, he adopted Angada, Vali's son by Tara.

Thus did Rama bring *dharma* to the land of the monkeys.

Hanuman, determined to overpower all his animal instincts, took the vow of celibacy and service. By the vow of celibacy, he sought to crush the desire for sensual gratification. By the vow of service, he sought to crush the desire to inflate the ego. When Rama learnt of Hanuman's decision, he was filled with awe and admiration for the monkey.

Sugriva, Hanuman and the residents of Kishkinda salute Rama, lord of civilisation; Andhra painting

36

Hanuman Leaps Across the Sea Chapter V

Lakshmana's Wrath

Soon after Sugriva's coronation, monsoon clouds covered the sky. Rains lashed the earth forcing the monkeys to seek shelter in caves. "We will start looking for Sita as soon as the rain stops," Sugriva promised Rama.

For four months, Rama and Lakshmana waited patiently as it poured incessantly. Finally, when the rain clouds departed, the brothers called upon Sugriva to keep his promise. The king of the *vanara*s, however, was too lost in royal revelry to bother with the search. This made Lakshmana very angry. He stormed into Kishkinda, bow in hand, determined to teach Sugriva a lesson.

Rama and Lakshmana wait for the rains to pass; Pahari painting

The monkeys were terrified. They ran to Hanuman who immediately requested Tara, the wise queen of the monkeys, to stall and pacify the hot-headed Lakshmana while he made Sugriva see the folly of his ways.

"Don't let the whirlpool of desires take you away from Rama. It will destroy you," Hanuman advised the monkey-king. Coming to his senses, Sugriva apologised to Rama and immediately set about making plans to find Sita.

Search for Sita

Search parties were organised to scour the southern half of Jambudvipa. Hanuman was made leader of one of the groups. He was joined by Angada, the son of Vali.

Before leaving, Rama gave Hanuman his signet ring. "When you find my beloved Sita, show this ring to her;

Sugriva apologises to Rama; painting from Andhra Pradesh

it will confirm your identity as my messenger. Should she doubt you, tell her that I still remember the time our eyes met in the royal garden of Mithila before I broke the divine bow of Shiva and won her hand in marriage. This is a secret that only Sita and I share."

As the monkeys moved away from Kishkinda towards the southern horizon, there was fear in their hearts because the south was the direction of Yama, god of death. He who went south, never returned. So it was said. So the monkeys believed.

The Nymph's Cave

For weeks Hanuman and his companions wandered south but found no trace of Sita. Jambuvan, the wise king of the *bhalukas* or bears, joined in their search. They spoke to animals, birds, serpents and other creatures of the forest. Many had seen Ravana's flying chariot, but none knew its final destination.

After moving over mountains, through valleys, across dense forests, wooded plains and thorny plateaux, Hanuman and his companions came upon a stretch of desert. Undaunted, they carried on.

For days they walked through the barren land without food or water. They would surely have died of thirst had Hanuman not spotted birds with wet wings leaving a cave. "There must be water in there," he said. The monkeys rushed in and found deep in the cavern a lake lined with trees bearing succulent fruits. They bathed in the lake, drank the water, ate the fruits and refreshed themselves.

Monkeys set out in all directions in search of Sita; North Indian painting

Hanuman spots birds with wet
wings leaving a cave; Pahari painting

Suddenly, a figure emerged at the far end of the lake,
startling the monkeys. It was a beautiful woman.
"Fear not. I am the *apsara* Swayamprabha," she said.
"Long ago, I was banished to this desolate cave by Indra,
king of the gods, because I helped his favourite nymph
elope with a demon. For centuries, I have longed for some
company. It appears the gods have finally answered my
prayers."

Hanuman Breaks Swayamprabha's Spell

Swayamprabha, the lonely nymph, was determined not
to lose the company of the monkeys. So she enchanted
them with her hospitality, offering them the choicest
of fruits and entertaining them with song, dance, riddles
and conversation. The monkeys enjoyed themselves so
much that they lost track of time. The cave became their
gilded prison.

Everyone, even the wise Jambuvan, succumbed to
Swayamprabha's charms and forgot all about the mission
to find Sita. But not Hanuman. As he prepared to leave,
the nymph tried to entice him too. "Forget about your
duty. Enjoy life. Marry and stay with me in my garden
forever. What more can any living creature wish for,"
she said.

Hanuman declined the offer. "I am on a mission to
find Sita. I shall carry on, with or without my
companions."

Moved by Hanuman's determination and realising the
seriousness of his mission, Swayamprabha let the
monkeys go, though with great reluctance. "Ravana's

39

Swayamprabha entertains the monkeys; painting from Rajasthan

kingdom stands on the island of Trikuta off the southern shore of Jambudvipa," she said. She gave directions, offered baskets of fruit for the long journey ahead and with tears in her eyes, bid the monkeys farewell.

For this act of generosity, Indra let Swayamprabha return to Amravati, the city of the gods.

The Southern Shore of Jambudvipa

The journey to the southern tip of Jambudvipa was a long and arduous one. By the time the monkeys saw the sea, they had finished all their supplies. Around them was no fruit-bearing tree; just a lifeless stretch of sand. Before them stood the ocean, green as emerald, stretching into the horizon. The island of Trikuta was somewhere beyond.

Hanuman and his companions sat on the beach, trying to figure out a way to locate Ravana's mysterious island-kingdom.

Days passed. Hungry and helpless, the monkeys groaned in despair. "We cannot turn back without information on Sita. We cannot move forward without directions to Lanka. What are we to do? Maybe we should sit on this beach and stare at the sea until our hearts stop beating."

Sampati, the Vulture

There lived on the southern coast of Jambudvipa an old vulture called Sampati who had no wings. When he saw the monkeys starving on the beach, he hobbled towards them, hoping they would die soon so that he could feed on their corpses.

As he waited patiently, he overheard the monkeys speak. Their conversations revolved around Rama, Ravana, Sita, Sugriva, Vali, Kishkinda, Ayodhya and Lanka. It did not interest him.

Then they mentioned Jatayu, the vulture who had died trying to stop Ravana from abducting Sita. Sampati's curiosity was greatly aroused, for Jatayu was his younger brother.

Sampati and Jatayu

When they were young, Jatayu and Sampati loved to fly together above the clouds. One day, Jatayu — in a fit of youthful passion — decided to test the power of his wings by flying towards the sun. His wings would surely have caught fire, had Sampati not shaded him with his own wings. In the event, Sampati's wings were singed and he lost the power of flight forever.

Sampati talks to Hanuman; Mughal miniature

Sampati learnt from Hanuman how Jatayu had come to Sita's rescue when she was being abducted by Ravana, how he had spread his wings and come in the way of the *rakshasa*'s flying chariot and how Ravana, determined to have his way, had sliced off his wings and left him to die on the forest floor.

Sampati Sees Lanka

Determined to avenge his brother's death, Sampati offered the monkeys his help in locating Ravana's island-kingdom. "I may not be able to fly, but I have keen eyesight, sharp enough to find Lanka even if it stands beyond the ends of the world," he told Hanuman.

Jatayu is killed as he tries to stop Ravana from abducting Sita; Pahari painting

Hanuman doubts his strength; Pahari painting

Sampati skewed his eyes to look beyond the southern horizon. After adjusting his eyes to the distance, he caught a glimpse of Lanka — its golden towers shrouded by mists glistened beyond the waves.

"I can see Lanka," he said, pointing in its direction. The monkeys cheered and clapped in excitement. "It is far away, almost a thousand miles from this shore. The sea between is deep, rough and full of serpents and monsters. Its walls are thick and its gate is guarded by Lankini, a fierce warrior-maiden, who never sleeps."

For helping the monkeys locate Lanka, the gods blessed Sampati and restored his wings so that he could fly for the rest of his days.

Hanuman's Self-doubt

The monkeys wondered how they could make their way to Lanka over a thousand miles of sea. "It is too far to swim," said one. "And the sea is too rough to sail," said another.

"We should ask Hanuman to leap across," suggested Jambuvan.

"I cannot do that," said Hanuman, "I am no bird. And even birds cannot fly that far."

The wise old bear knew the reason for Hanuman's self-doubt. It made him smile.

When Hanuman was a child, he used his strength recklessly. In a spirit of play, he often scared wild elephants making them run amuck in the forests, destroying everything in their path, even hermitages of forest-sages and their sacrificial altars. Unable to deprive Hanuman of his strength, the sages cast a spell that made Hanuman forget much of his powers. "His memory will return when the time is right," they said.

"Now is the time when your strength is needed in the service of Rama," said Jambuvan. Instantly, Hanuman regained memory of his divine strength and prepared to make the journey to Lanka

Hanuman Begins his Journey

As Hanuman mustered the strength, his body began to grow in size, expanding to enormous proportions.
His face glowed like the rising sun. Energy throbbed through his powerful limbs. His eyes blazed like comets.
His breath rumbled like an impatient volcano.
His upraised tail resembled the banner of Kartikeya, the celestial warlord.

All those who saw him trembled in fear. Birds took to the sky, lions hid in caves, crabs slipped under the sand.

Hanuman climbed to the peak of Mount Mahendra that stood overlooking the southern sea. With a hoot that stunned wild elephants, he sprang to the sky. The impulse of his leap flattened the mountain.

Clouds parted to make way for the son of Vayu.
Sea-creatures rose to the surface to watch Hanuman make his way across the sky.

As he flew, Hanuman touched the bright stars above and admired the shimmering sea below. He saw fishes, serpents, turtles and whales raising their heads to catch a glimpse of him.

Hanuman, Angada and Jambuvan climbing mount Mahendra;
Pahari painting

Hanuman leaps into the sky;
Pahari painting

Hanuman Outwits Surasa

Midway between Jambudvipa and Lanka, a great monster with huge jaws and sharp teeth blocked Hanuman's path. It was Surasa, the mother of snakes.

The gods had ordained that no creature could cross the southern sea without entering Surasa's mouth. No creature that entered her mouth ever left it alive. This was the reason why no human, bird, beast or reptile had ever made its way to Ravana's island-kingdom.

Realising he could not bypass Surasa, Hanuman increased his size to make it difficult for Surasa to swallow him. Surasa, however, widened her jaws to accommodate the flying monkey. Hanuman kept growing bigger and bigger and Surasa's mouth kept getting wider and wider.

Then, Hanuman reduced his size to that of a mosquito, zoomed into Surasa's mouth and out — all in a blink of the eye.

"There I have entered your mouth. Now let me pass," he said. Realising she had been outwitted, Surasa had no choice but to comply. Impressed by Hanuman's quick thinking, Surasa showered him with blessings.

Hanuman enters Surasa's mouth; painting from Rajasthan

Simhika trying to eat Hanuman;
illustration from Gujarat

Hanuman Kills Simhika

As Hanuman made his way over the sea, he cast a vast
shadow on the waters that caught the attention of
Simhika, an eel-like dragon who caught her prey by
casting a spell on their shadow.

Spellbound, Hanuman found himself being sucked into
Simhika's mouth. As the jaws snapped shut, Hanuman
was trapped in her throat.

Before the dragon could release her digestive juices,
Hanuman stretched out his hand and squeezed her heart.
Simhika writhed in agony and died. Hanuman ripped
open the dragon's belly with his sharp nails and emerged
out unscathed.

Simhika's blood oozed into the sea, turning it red.

After washing the gore that covered his body, Hanuman
resumed his flight, cheered by fishes, serpents, turtles,
whales and other sea creatures.

Mainaka's Help

Not far from Lanka, a mountain rose from the sea and
obstructed Hanuman's path. The mountain identified
itself as Mainaka, son of the Himalayas. "Come rest on
my peak. Refresh yourself with the fruits that grow on my
slopes before you continue your journey."

45

Mount Mainaka asks Hanuman to rest; Rajasthani painting

Long ago, mountains had wings and their movement across the sky disturbed the sages who lived on earth. In response to sages' pleas, Indra went about plucking out the wings of mountains. To save himself, Mainaka hid himself under the sea and had kept himself hidden until he saw Hanuman flying above. "The pleasure of serving you, the servant of Rama, is greater than the risk of being discovered by Indra," said Mainaka.

Hanuman thanked Mainaka for his kindness but politely refused the offer of hospitality. "I cannot rest until I find Sita," he said and continued on his way.

The City of Lanka

At long last, having crossed a thousand miles of sea, Hanuman saw the island of Trikuta on the horizon. Above was the sapphire blue sky. Below was the emerald green sea. In between stood a grand citadel of gold with bright red banners fluttering atop every tower. It was Lanka!

Vishvakarma, the architect of the gods, had built this city to befit the grandeur of the *yaksha*-king Kubera, its original ruler. Moulded out of gold, it was more beautiful than Amravati, the abode of the gods.

Since the day the *rakshasa*-king Ravana had driven Kubera away and usurped the throne of Lanka, few mortal eyes had feasted upon the splendour of this amazing island-kingdom. Hanuman knew this as he walked on the shores of Trikuta, admiring the dazzling arches, the radiant towers and the gem-studded gates.

The sheer splendour of Ravana's city left Hanuman speechless. If this was the beauty of the city on the outside, what would it be on the inside, he wondered.

Hanuman reaches Lanka; illustration by author

Hanuman Finds Sita

Chapter VI

The Story of Trikuta

Ravana's golden city Lanka stood on an island that was in fact the tip of an undersea mountain called Trikuta. Trikuta was once a peak of Meru, the mountain that stands in the centre of the universe.

Aeons ago, the wind-god Vayu and the serpent-king Vasuki were involved in a test of strength. Vayu was attempting to blow away Trikuta while Vasuki held it in place by coiling around the base of the mountain.

The two were equally matched. Determined to win, Vayu whipped up a storm whose fury troubled the gods. "Stop you two," they cried, "Before the cosmic scaffold comes tumbling down."

Vasuki immediately relaxed his grip. Taking advantage of this situation, Vayu swept away Trikuta and dropped it into the southern ocean. Its tip formed an island.

As the island came into being because of deceit, the gods decreed that only demons would live on it.

To make amends, Vayu promised he would father the warrior who would crush the demons of Trikuta. That warrior was Hanuman.

Lankini, guardian-goddess of Lanka; wood carving from South India

Hanuman Defeats Lankini

When Hanuman landed on Trikuta, it was midnight. All the *rakshasas* were asleep. Only Lankini stomped outside the walls of Lanka. She never slept.

Lankini was a warrior-maiden who once guarded the abode of Brahma, father of all living creatures, until she was cursed for her arrogance. "You will guard the city of demons until a monkey defeats you," Brahma said.

Lankini had blazing eyes and mighty arms bearing weapons of every description. She blocked Hanuman's entry into Ravana's city. "Identify yourself," she said.

Impatient to pass through the gates, Hanuman revealed his gigantic form. His head reached the celestial realms, his feet stretched into the nether regions. His tail lashed the sea to whip up a storm. His eyes flashed thunder and he breathed out fire. He let out a piercing war cry, terrifying Lankini.

"You are none other than Rudra, the howling destroyer," she cried and ran away, leaving Lanka unguarded.

Hanuman terrifies Lankini with his giant form; modern illustration

Inside Lanka

Under cover of darkness, Hanuman entered Lanka, reducing himself to the size of a bee so that he could fly unnoticed through the city of *rakshasa*s.

He moved through the tree-lined avenues, across well-lit squares, admiring golden mansions, gem-studded palaces, painted pavilions and perfumed groves. He found deer in every garden, fishes in every pond, birds on every tree. Where in this maze of a beautiful city was Sita, he wondered.

He searched every house and garden until he came upon Ravana's palace.

Ravana's Harem

Ravana's palace stood in a flowery meadow. It had bright red gates, pillars of gold and walls with frescoes of flower-laden creepers and colourful birds. The light of torches bounced off the crystal floor. Gem-encrusted tapestries and fresh water fountains reflected the moonlight. Gateways guided the cool breeze into passages and courtyards.

Hanuman flew into the palace and found servants, slaves, guards, cooks, dancers, queens, concubines, princes and princesses sleeping peacefully.

Right in the centre of the palace complex, on a gigantic bed, he found Ravana in the arms of several beautiful women. These were the wives of warriors and sages, who had abandoned their husbands in favour of Ravana.

Which one of them was Sita, Hanuman wondered. He brushed this thought aside for he knew the wife of Rama would never renounce her chastity.

48 Ravana and his queens; Chitrakathi painting from Maharashtra

Mandodari, the Frog-lady

At the first light of dawn, the palace began to stir.

In the inner chambers, Hanuman came upon a serene lady who had kept an all-night vigil, chanting hymns and praying for Ravana's wellbeing. It was Mandodari, the chief queen. Renowned in the three worlds for her chastity, she stood by her husband despite all his faults, earning the adoration of the gods.

Mandodari and Ravana; Phad painting from Gujarat

Long ago, Ravana had heard that Parvati, wife of the hermit-god Shiva was the most beautiful woman in the world. Desirous of possessing her, he performed austerities to please Shiva. The hermit-god who was detached from all things including his wife, permitted Ravana to take Parvati to Lanka.

Parvati was not amused by what had transpired between her husband and Ravana. She forgave Shiva because he was a simpleton but decided to teach Ravana a lesson. She caught hold of a female frog or *manduka* and with her divine powers transformed it into a beautiful woman called Mandodari. Ravana mistook this woman to be Parvati, carried her off to his island-kingdom and made her his chief queen.

Like all female frogs, Mandodari demanded her husband's company only at the start of the rainy season. But she was a faithful wife offering her unworthy husband sound advice and unconditional support.

Mandodari's Daughter

Mandodari's handmaidens were busy gossiping about Sita. Hanuman noticed that every time the name Sita was mentioned, Mandodari's breasts oozed milk. He wondered why.

Not long after marrying Mandodari, Ravana decided to perform a grand *yagna* using the blood of sages as the sacrificial offering. *Rishi*s were beheaded and their blood collected in a jar that Ravana gave to Mandodari for safekeeping.

One night, Mandodari woke up feeling very thirsty and accidentally drank the contents of the jar. The blood of the sages entered her body and made her pregnant. In due course, she gave birth to a daughter. Oracles revealed that the child would be the cause of Ravana's death.

To save her husband, Mandodari had the child thrown into the sea. The sea-god Varuna saved Mandodari's daughter and gave her into the care of the earth-goddess who in turn handed her over to Janaka, king of Videha, who named the child Sita.

49

The Woman Under the Ashoka Tree

As the sun appeared on the horizon, Hanuman entered a pleasure-garden located at the far end of Ravana's palace. There, under an Ashoka tree, he found a woman looking forlorn. A large number of warrior-women watched over her.

Some of the women were taunting her: "You fool, forget your husband and marry Ravana." Some were cajoling her: "Don't be shy. Bedeck yourself with the jewels he has offered you and go to him joyfully." Some were threatening her, "Do not try his patience. He will eat you alive."

The woman under the Ashoka tree ignored them all. Her face was calm, her will unshakeable.

Hanuman realised he had stumbled upon Sita.

Hanuman finds Sita being harassed by her guards; painting from Andhra Pradesh

Sita Stands up to Ravana

In the morning, to the sound of conches, Ravana entered the pleasure-garden with a garland round his neck, on a golden palanquin, surrounded by finely dressed minions.

"Well, my dear Sita, will you come to my chambers tonight. Look, I have brought you a gift that will help you make up your mind." So saying, Ravana threw the cut head of Rama in her direction. "Now you no longer have to bother with marital fidelity. I have killed Rama. You are a free woman."

The women gasped but Sita remained unmoved. She threw the 'head' which was in fact a coconut back at Ravana. "Your sorcery does not fool me. Had this really been Rama's head, I would not have been alive to see it; my heart would have stopped beating the very moment he died."

50 Ravana threatening Sita; painting from Rajasthan

Annoyed by his failure, Ravana said, "If you do not come voluntarily, I will make you mine by force."

Unfazed by the threat, Sita picked up a blade of grass and placed it between herself and Ravana. "You cross this blade of grass and I swear, by the strength of my chastity, your head will burst into a thousand pieces."

Powerless before Sita's unwavering virtue, Ravana left in a huff.

The warrior-women continued taunting, cajoling and threatening Sita.

Hanuman Presents Himself

After Ravana had departed, Hanuman decided it was time to present himself. Late in the afternoon, when the warrior-women were taking a nap, he dropped Rama's signet ring before Sita, arousing her curiosity.

When she looked up, she saw a golden monkey saluting her. "I am Hanuman, son of Vayu, Sugriva's minister and Rama's messenger," he said.

Sita suspected this was yet another *rakshasa* disguised as a monkey sent by Ravana to play tricks with her mind. To remove these doubts, Hanuman told her the secret known only to her and Rama: "Before Rama broke the divine bow of Shiva and won your hand in marriage, you saw him in the garden of your father's palace and your eyes met."

Convinced of the monkey's identity, Sita smiled — the first time since her abduction. "My lord has not forgotten me."

Hanuman alighted from the tree and bowed at her feet.

51

Indrajit, son of Ravana; temple wall carving from Indonesia

"No, he has not. In fact, he has raised an army and will soon come to Lanka, kill Ravana and rescue you." Hanuman's words gladdened Sita's heart. "If you wish, you can climb on my back and I will carry you over the sea to Rama."

Sita declined the offer for she wanted Rama to do his husbandly duty and liberate her after killing the man who had dared dishonour him.

"I shall tell him of your desire. Before I go, kindly give me something as proof our meeting."

Sita gave Hanuman her jewel-studded hairpin. "Tell my lord, I anxiously await his triumphant arrival."

Destruction of the Pleasure-Garden

His mission complete, Hanuman prepared to leave Lanka. But he did not want to go without teaching Ravana a lesson or two.

He decided to vandalise the pleasure-garden where Sita was being held prisoner. He leapt from tree to tree, squashing the flowers and crushing the fruits. He pulled out the ferns and uprooted the trees. He muddied the pool and scared away the birds.

When warrior-women who guarded Sita tried to shoo him away, he scratched their faces, pulled their hair and broke their weapons.

The royal guards were summoned, but they were no match for the agile Hanuman.

When news of the vandalism reached Ravana, he dispatched his young son Akshaya to capture the miscreant. Eager to prove his valour, the young prince entered the garden in his chariot and shot an arrow at Hanuman. Hanuman, in turn, hurled a rock and smashed Akshaya's skull.

Indrajit Captures Hanuman

The death of Akshaya at the hands of a monkey alarmed Ravana who sent Meghanath, his eldest son, to capture the trouble-maker.

Meghanath was the most powerful warrior in Lanka with many victories to his credit. He had even defeated Indra in battle, earning the title of Indrajit, vanquisher of the king of the gods.

Indrajit soon discovered that the monkey in the garden was no ordinary beast; he was agile enough to dodge the sticks and stones thrown at him, nimble enough to slip out of nets and avoid capture. Exasperated, he was forced to raise his bow and shoot arrows at the monkey.

Hanuman caught in the serpent-rope; illustration by author

Vibhishana leaves Ravana's court where Hanuman is made fun of; painting from Andhra Pradesh

But even this failed because the monkey simply caught the missiles and broke them before they could touch him.

Indrajit finally shot the *Brahmastra*, an arrow reverberating with the power of Brahma. The arrow had the power to kill a god; it only stunned Hanuman.

When Hanuman fell down, Indrajit bound him with *nagapasha* — self-coiling magical serpent-ropes — and dragged him into Ravana's court.

Vibhishana Speaks Out

All the residents of Lanka gathered in Ravana's court to see the monkey who had killed Akshaya and confounded Indrajit.

When Ravana had taken his seat, cheered by the *rakshasa*s, Hanuman identified himself. "I am Hanuman, son of Vayu, Sugriva's minister and messenger of Sita's husband Rama."

At the mention of Rama's name, a stunned silence descended upon the court. "You are no messenger. You are a monkey," hissed Ravana and the whole court burst out laughing.

Only Vibhishana did not laugh. Vibhishana was Ravana's younger brother who had repeatedly counselled against the abduction of Rama's wife. "Only barbarians do not respect the law of marriage," he had told his brother, "Return Sita to her husband." Needless to say, Ravana did not heed his words.

"Brother, let us hear what this monkey has to say," pleaded Vibhishana.

"Shut up or get out, Vibhishana," yelled Ravana. The courtiers stifled a giggle. Humiliated, Vibhishana bowed his head and left the court.

53

Ravana ordering his soldiers to set Hanuman's tail on fire; illustration by author

A Throne for Hanuman

"Well, untie these ropes and offer me seat. Don't you *rakshasas* know how to extend courtesy that is due to a messenger," said Hanuman

"A cage in the royal zoo will suit you better," said Indrajit. Ravana and all the *rakshasas* roared in laughter.

Hanuman was not amused. Since he was not offered a seat, he decided to make a seat for himself.

First, he puffed his chest and split the *nagapasha* that bound him. Then, he lengthened his tail, coiled it around to make a tower, leapt on it and sat down looking down upon Ravana. "A seat higher than Ravana's throne befits Rama's messenger," he said much to Ravana's irritation.

Hanuman Slaps Ravana

"Better let go of Sita or Rama will destroy your golden city when he comes to rescue his wife," warned Hanuman.

Ravana lost his temper at Hanuman's open display of irreverence. He began abusing Rama. "Rama has no right over Sita. He left her unguarded, free for the taking and I took her as the law of the jungle permits."

"Then you are just a beast, nothing more." So saying, Hanuman raised his hand and — as the *rakshasa*-court watched in horror — slapped Ravana so hard that his crown fell to the floor. Hanuman grabbed the crown and threw it away.

Frothing with fury, Ravana ordered his *rakshasas* to set Hanuman's tail on fire.

Hanuman raising his hand as if to slap Ravana; temple carving from Karnataka

54

Hanuman's Burning Tail

The *rakshasa*s pounced upon Hanuman, pinned him to the ground and dragged him to the city-square where strips of oil-soaked rags were wrapped round his tail and set alight. Everyone was excited at the prospect of watching the monkey with a burning tail squirm and suffer.

But Hanuman had other plans.

As soon as the tail was set on fire, he pushed the *rakshasa*s away, jumped up to the roof, swung his burning tail around and set the tapestries ablaze. Soon the ceiling of Ravana's palace was on fire leading to pandemonium.

Some *rakshasa*s rushed to fetch water to put out the blaze. Others ran to catch Hanuman before he did more damage. As the fire spread, Ravana's queens ran out of

Pandemonium in Lanka as Hanuman carries off Ravana's crown; Mughal miniature painting

the palace, screaming and shouting. Children began to cry. The horses in the stables went berserk.

Lanka Ablaze

Hanuman, meanwhile, flew out of the palace, leapt from roof to roof, swinging his burning tail and setting each and every building in Lanka on fire.

Soon all the palaces, mansions, pavilions, orchards and avenues of Ravana's city — except Sita's garden and Vibhishana's home — were engulfed in flames. The gold began to melt. Pillars crumbled, walls collapsed, roofs crashed.

Indrajit shot an arrow into the sky forcing the clouds to shed rain. But nothing could put out the inferno.

Helpless, the *rakshasa*s ran to the streets to save themselves. Standing amidst the columns of smoke, they cursed the moment they set eyes on Hanuman.

As Ravana watched Hanuman fly off towards Jambudvipa, his laughter ringing in the air, he realised he had just been subjected to his first taste of Rama's might. More would surely follow.

Hanuman sets Lanka ablaze; illustration by author

Hanuman Builds the Bridge Chapter VII

Return to Kishkinda

When Hanuman, Angada and Jambuvan returned to Kishkinda, their mission complete, they were treated to a grand welcome.

Baskets of fruits and cups of honey were passed around as Hanuman described their perilous journey to the edge of Jambudvipa and his flight across the southern sea. The monkeys were spellbound by the adventures on the way and the descriptions of Lanka's beauty. They let out whoops of victory when Hanuman narrated how he outfoxed the *rakshasa*s and burnt their city.

Hanuman allayed the anxiety in Rama's heart by describing his meeting with Sita. When he presented Sita's hairpin, Rama's eyes were filled with tears; he embraced the monkey who had filled his heart with hope and determination.

Then, cheered by birds, the monkeys of Kishkinda led by Sugriva, Angada and Hanuman prepared to do battle with Ravana. Jambuvan joined them with a contingent of bears. Everyone followed Rama as he made his way to the coast, determined to crush the ten-headed Lord of Lanka.

Chapter VII

Hanuman shares his adventures in Lanka with Rama; Mysore painting

Rama and his army of monkeys; Temple wall carving from South India

Hanuman outwits Benjkaya;
Thai painting

Benjkaya, the Sorceress

When Rama reached the southern edge of Jambudvipa, he saw the green waters of the ocean stretching into the horizon. Beyond stood Lanka, the island-kingdom of Ravana. Locked somewhere within its golden citadel was his beloved Sita.

From the highest tower of his palace, Ravana saw Rama and his army of monkeys assembling on the beach. Alarmed, he thought of a plan that would force Rama to turn back.

On his orders, the sorceress Benjkaya took the form of a corpse, cast herself adrift on the ocean and let herself be washed ashore, not far from where the monkeys were gathering. When the corpse was brought before Rama, he recognised the necklace on it as that belonging to Sita.

"Ravana must have killed Sita and thrown her body into the sea," he cried. Lamenting the loss of his beloved, he fell to the ground heartbroken.

Hanuman felt something was amiss. He ordered his monkeys to place the corpse on a pile of wood and lit the funeral pyre. As soon as fire engulfed the corpse, it jumped up and began to run towards the sea. Hanuman caught hold of the 'dead body' and forced the sorceress to reveal all to Rama or risk a painful punishment.

Benjkaya fell at Hanuman's feet and begged for forgiveness. "Make me your wife. I cannot return to Lanka and I have no where else to go." Hanuman declined the offer but promised her shelter and protection.

The sorceress spent the rest of her life in Kishkinda singing praises of the wise and compassionate monkey.

Vibhishana Joins Rama

As Rama wondered how he could get his monkey troops across the sea, news came that a demon from Lanka was heading their way.

Picking up his bow, Lakshmana rushed to the beach. Sure enough, a *rakshasa* could be seen flying towards Jambudvipa.

"Shall I shoot him down?" asked Lakshmana. "No, don't," said Hanuman. "I recognise him. It is Vibhishana, Ravana's younger brother. In Ravana's court, he was the only one who said that Sita should be allowed to return to her husband."

Ravana had banished Vibhishana from Lanka for speaking out against the abduction of Sita. Vibhishana now sought to join forces with Rama.

Vibhishana befriends Rama;
Mysore painting

Vibhishana approaches Rama; painting from Rajasthan

"How can I trust a man who is willing to fight his own brother?" asked Rama. Vibhishana replied, "I join you not to fight my brother but to fight the man who seeks to impose the law of the jungle on human society."

Pleased with this reply, Rama let Vibhishana join his army.

Promise of the Sea-god

Rama pondered over the problem of getting his army across the sea to Lanka. They could not fly like Hanuman. It was too far to swim. And there were not enough trees around to build ships. There were only stones.

Desperate, Rama raised his bow and prepared to shoot a lethal arrow to force Varuna, the sea-god, to part the waters. "Stop," said Varuna appearing before Rama.

Monkeys build the bridge to Lanka; modern illustration

59

Hanuman and the mermaid Svarna-matsya; Thai painting

"The waters will not part but will keep stones afloat. That will enable you to build a bridge to Lanka."

Pleased with the sea-god's response Rama lowered his bow. But since the arrow had been mounted it had to be released. "Shoot it in the opposite direction," said Hanuman. Rama shot the arrow to the North — the place where it struck the earth became a desert now known as Thar.

Rama ordered his monkey troop to build a bridge to Lanka. The monkey Nila designed the bridge; Hanuman was the overseer.

Before the stones were flung, Hanuman would carve the name 'Rama' on the stones with his nails. "Let the rocks reverberate with the power of Rama, upholder of righteousness."

The Mermaid Queen

Taking the name of Rama, the monkeys gathered stones and hurled them into the sea under the watchful eye of Hanuman and Nila. Unfortunately, enthusiasm dampened when the stones flung into the sea did not stay together. They would drift away in all directions.

Hanuman decided to investigate. He dived into the sea and found the fishes were responsible for dismantling the bridge. Hanuman shook his tail vigorously and agitated the waters, paralysing all the fishes.

He then confronted Svarna-matsya, the golden mermaid, queen of the fishes and demanded an explanation. "I was ordered by Ravana to do so," she replied. "But why are you involved in this battle between Rama and Ravana? You, who are so strong, handsome and intelligent, should enjoy your life instead. Marry me Hanuman. Together we can rule the sea, unconcerned with the cares of the world above."

"What use is my strength, beauty and wisdom if they only serve me. I live for others, not to indulge my senses or inflate my ego." So saying Hanuman declined Svarna-matsya's offer and rose to the surface.

Sea monsters prevent monkeys from building the bridge to Lanka; temple wall carving from Bali in Indonesia

Five-headed Hanuman in his fierce form; Kangra painting

Rama and his army of monkeys cross the bridge to Lanka; Mughal painting

Impressed by Hanuman's selflessness, the mermaid queen ordered all the creatures of the sea to disobey Ravana and to help in the building of Rama's bridge.

The fishes, the serpents, the seals and sea-monsters held the stones together and the bridge to Lanka finally took shape.

Hanuman Bridges the Gap

When the bridge was complete, Rama and Lakshmana blew their war conches and saluted Durga, the goddess of war. Hanuman let out a war-cry, filling the heart of every monkey with confidence, and led the monkey troop over the bridge across the sea to Lanka.

As the monkeys approached their destination, Ravana hurled two missiles and destroyed the two ends of the bridge. Rama and his monkey troop were thus stranded on sea, unable to cross over to Lanka or return to Jambudvipa.

Before this calamity could sap the motivation of the monkeys, Hanuman came up with a plan. He increased his size and stretched himself over the gap, placing his hands on the shore of Lanka and his feet on the edge of the bridge. The monkeys scrambled over his back and reached Ravana's island kingdom.

As Rama walked over Hanuman's back, Hanuman said, "I am blessed today for I have been touched by the feet of Rama."

Rama Reaches Lanka

As soon as they stepped on the shores of Lanka, the monkeys and bears of Rama's army noticed that the city Hanuman had burnt down had been rebuilt and restored to its former glory. "To be able to do this so quickly, the *rakshasa*s must have magical powers," said Jambuvan, scaring one and all.

"They may have magic, but we have righteousness on our side," said Hanuman restoring confidence amongst the *vanara*s and *bhaluka*s.

On his orders the monkeys and the bears began to growl menacingly, challenging the *rakshasa*s to a fight. The rumbling sound filled the air and frightened the residents of Lanka. "It is the menagerie of doom," declared the oracles.

The Battle Begins

"Give up Sita, she is someone else's wife," cried some *rakshasa*s. "Make peace, before our civilisation is destroyed," implored others.

Ravana informed of Rama's arrival on the shores of Lanka; Mughal painting

Hanuman smashes the war-chariots of *rakshasa*s; Pahari painting

Ravana was in no mood to listen. "They are monkeys and bears. We will hunt them down. Their heads will be trophies on our halls. Their skin will be clothing for our wives. Their flesh will be food for our children. Come, mount your chariots, wear your armours, pick your weapons, let loose your hunting dogs. Let us drive Rama's rabble away."

To the sound of bugles, the gates of Ravana's citadel opened and a hundred wild hunting dogs rushed out followed by fierce *rakshasa*s mounted on war-chariots.

At first, the monkeys and bears were scared. But then, Hanuman picked up a stone and hurled it at the *rakshasa* leading the attack, knocking him dead. A whoop of victory rose from the monkey army. Gaining confidence, they rushed onwards with sticks and stones, determined to overpower Ravana's grand army.

Carnage of War

The bears frightened away the dogs and startled the horses. The monkeys leapt into chariots, kicking, punching and biting the *rakshasa*s into submission.

Rama rode into battle on Hanuman while Lakshmana rode on Angada. They shot arrows while their troops showered sticks and stones on Ravana's army.

Rama rides into battle on Hanuman's shoulders; illustration by author

Soon the battlefield was enveloped in dust. Blood of *vanara*s, *bhaluka*s and *rakshasa*s covered the ground. The air was filled with the din of drums, bugles and war-cries.

Banners were torn, chariots were smashed and weapons cast asunder. Bones were broken, flesh was torn, eyes were gouged out, as the *vanara*s went on the offensive. Vultures circled in the sky above.

Hanuman Dances on Ravana's Head

As the day of battle drew to a close, Ravana stood on the highest tower of Lanka to survey the results. He saw his troops being driven back into his citadel. He feared that ancient prophecy of sages would probably come true: he would face defeat at the hands of monkeys.

Hanuman saw Ravana standing on the tower. He took a giant leap and landed on Ravana's head. To the shock of *rakshasa*s and the amusement of *vanara*s and *bhaluka*s, he danced on Ravana, kicking his crowns to the ground.

The monkeys roared their approval. The *rakshasa*s remained silent in shame.

Hanuman dances on Ravana's head; illustration by author

Garuda to the Rescue

Ravana's son Indrajit led the *rakshasa*-army into the battlefield. He hurled his dreaded serpent-ropes called *nagapasha* at Rama and Lakshmana. The ropes coiled around the brothers' neck, choking until they lost consciousness.

"Only the divine eagle Garuda, eternal enemy of serpents, can break these ropes and release the brothers," said Jambuvan. The king of the bears invoked the mighty bird who descended from the heavens flapping his golden wings.

Rama and Lakshmana trapped in Indrajit's serpent-ropes; Pahari painting

Hanuman and Garuda locked in combat; modern illustration

Mistaking Garuda for a demon, Hanuman rose to the sky and wrestled him mid-air. "Stop," cried the sun. "Don't you recognise Garuda, Vishnu's mount," he said addressing Hanuman.

Offering his apologies, Hanuman led Garuda to the brothers. With his sharp beak and talons, Garuda pecked out the *nagapasha* and released Rama and Lakshmana from its death-grip. The brothers thanked their saviour who then returned to Vaikuntha, the abode of Vishnu.

The Illusion of Sita

Indrajit came up with a plan to demotivate Rama and make him return to Jambudvipa. He hovered over the battlefield in Ravana's flying chariot and created an illusion of Sita.

As Rama watched in horror, Indrajit slit Sita's throat and she slumped down dead. Having seen the unimaginable, Rama lost his will to fight. He collapsed on the floor and lamented the loss of his wife. Lakshmana, Sugriva and Jambuvan tried to console him in vain.

Hanuman, however, suspected something was amiss. Taking the form of a bee, he flew into Lanka and found Sita safe under the Ashoka tree in Ravana's pleasure-garden, praying for Rama's victory. "How do I convince Rama that you are alive?" he asked Sita.

Sita replied, "Tell Rama the story that only he and I know. While wandering in the forest, a crow kept harassing me by pulling my hair and pecking my cheek. Furious, my lord put out one of his eyes with a blade of grass."

Rama in despair when he believes the lie that Sita has been killed; Pahari painting

When Hanuman narrated this story to Rama, he was sure his beloved was alive. Angry at the trick Indrajit had played on him, Rama raised his bow and shot arrows that forced Indrajit to seek refuge behind Lanka's walls.

The giant Kumbhakarna is woken up; North Indian painting

Kumbhakarna Roused

Indrajit's defeat at the hands of Rama set Ravana thinking. He realised Rama was more powerful than he imagined. He needed reinforcements to ensure his victory. He decided to wake up Kumbhakarna.

Kumbhakarna was Ravana's younger brother and a giant. He was so strong that he could raise a whirlwind by simply sneezing. When he invoked Brahma, father of all living creatures, to secure a boon that would make him more powerful, the gods were alarmed. At their request, Saraswati, the goddess of speech, twisted Kumbhakarna's tongue so that he accidentally asked Brahma for the boon of eternal sleep. Ravana came to his brother's rescue and managed to modify the boon so that Kumbhakarna woke up for one day a year. "On that day, even the gods will not be able to defeat him in battle," said Brahma. "Be warned, however, should he be roused from his sleep on any other day, he will surely meet his death."

Impatient to have his giant brother fight on his behalf, Ravana ignored Brahma's warning and sent his attendants to wake up Kumbhakarna.

Trumpets were blown into the giant's ears, brooms were used to tickle his nose, buckets of water were poured on his face, spears were poked into his soles, forcing him out of his deep slumber.

Kumbhakarna goes into battle; Tanjore painting

67

Death of Kumbhakarna

On hearing the events that had transpired while he was asleep, Kumbhakarna felt that Ravana was wrong to abduct another man's wife. He, however, agreed to fight Rama.

Kumbhakarna entered the battlefield. When he saw Vibhishana fighting beside Rama, he was furious. "What ever be Ravana's fault, he is our brother. By fighting for his enemy you have turned against your family. Your treachery disgusts me." So saying, he rushed towards Vibhishana who took refuge behind Rama.

Kumbhakarna's eyes were like cartwheels; his teeth like elephant tusks. On his approach, the monkeys retreated in terror.

Hanuman rushed forwards and faced Kumbhakarna. With a giant leap, he landed on the giant's shoulder and bit off his ear.

When the monkeys heard Kumbhakarna howl in pain, they realised the giant was not invulnerable. They turned back and scrambled over Kumbhakarna's legs like a swarm of locusts. They scratched his eyes, yanked his hair, wrenched his nose, broke his teeth, split his lip, bit his chin, and kicked his shin. Kumbhakarna tried to shake them off but failed.

While Kumbhakarna was thus distracted, Rama's arrows pierced and cut his limbs. He fell like an ancient fig tree. The ground shook.

When the dust had settled, the giant expressed his final wish. "Please do not let the *rakshasa*s see my body

Monkeys attack Kumbhakarna; Mughal painting

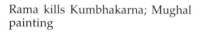

Rama kills Kumbhakarna; Mughal painting

Lakshmana battles Indrajit; Mughal painting

thus mutilated by monkeys. The shame and guilt will be too much for Ravana to bear." Accordingly, Hanuman picked up Kumbhakarna's corpse, carried it to the beach and hurled it into the sea.

Indrajit Shoots Lakshmana Down

The death of Kumbhakarna was a severe blow to the *rakshasa* morale. Determined to crush the *vanaras*, Indrajit marched out with a mighty army.

He fought with a fury that was never seen before on the battlefield. By the time the sun was overhead, the dead bodies of scores of monkeys and bears littered the battlefield.

Lakshmana challenged Indrajit to a duel and the two shot arrows at each other. Just as the sun was about to set, Indrajit shot a poison-tipped arrow that pierced Lakshmana on the shoulders. Instantly, Lakshmana's skin turned blue and he fell down unconscious.

Indrajit returned to Lanka to a hero's welcome. The *vanaras* and *bhalukas* gathered around Lakshmana to see if he was dead or alive.

Hanuman Fetches the Doctor

Holding Lakshmana in his arms, Rama cried, "Oh brother, my brother. I promised your mother Sumitra that I would look after your welfare. Now, how will I show her my face."

Hanuman could not bear to see Rama suffer thus. "How can I help?" he asked Vibhishana. Vibhishana instructed Hanuman to fetch Sushena, a skilled *rakshasa*-physician, who lived in Lanka.

"Will he help Ravana's enemy?" asked Jambuvan.

"He is a doctor — he does not discriminate between patients," replied Vibhishana.

Hanuman fetches the doctor Sushena to save Lakshmana; illustration by author

69

Hanuman immediately took the form of a bee, flew into Lanka and following directions given by Vibhishana found the *rakshasa*-physician. Not wanting to risk rejection, he uprooted Sushena's house from its foundation and carried him over the walls of Lanka to where Lakshmana lay unconscious.

Sushena examined Lakshmana and said, "The poison on the tip of Indrajit's arrow is spreading rapidly through his body. The only herb that can act as an antidote is *Sanjivani* that grows on Gandhamadana, a hill that stands south of Mount Kailasa in the Himalayas. Fetch if before the setting of the moon and the rising of the sun, and I will be able to save his life."

Hanuman Meets Bharata

Hanuman set out North to fetch the life-saving *Sanjivani*. With lightening speed, he crossed the sea and travelled over Kishkinda, Dandaka and Vindhya to enter Aryavarta.

As he flew over Kosala, the residents of Ayodhya mistook him for a flying monster. To allay their anxiety, Bharata shot an arrow and forced Hanuman to descend to the ground.

"Identify yourself," said Bharata. When Hanuman identified himself and explained his mission, Bharata could not believe his ears. Embracing Hanuman, he said "Dear friend, I am Bharata, Rama's ill-fated brother. I had no idea of Rama's misadventure. I wish I could help him out of in this hour of need, but alas, I cannot leave Ayodhya."

"If you can help me reach Gandhamadana rapidly and make up for lost time, that would be more than enough," Hanuman said.

Bharata helping Hanuman reach Gandhamadana on time; North Indian painting

"That I can do." So saying Bharata mounted an arrow on his bow and asked Hanuman to sit on the arrowhead. Chanting a *mantra*, he shot the arrow with such speed that it ripped through the clouds and reached the foot of Gandhamadana in the blink of an eye.

Kalanemi

On the slopes of Gandhamadana, Hanuman found a sage meditating. "Can you tell me where I can find the herb called *Sanjivani*?"

"Yes, I will," said the sage. "But you cannot touch it with unwashed hands. There is a lake behind my hermitage. Bathe in it, wash off the dirt that covers your body and then I will tell you where the herb grows."

Hanuman did as the sage advised. Unknown to him, a huge crocodile lived in the lake. As soon as Hanuman entered the water, the crocodile came up to him stealthily, opened its jaws and swallowed him up. To escape, Hanuman expanded himself until he burst out of the crocodile's belly.

The crocodile turned out to be a charming nymph. Hanuman had liberated her from the curse that had turned her into a reptile.

The nymph warned Hanuman, "The sage who directed you to this lake is Kalanemi, a magician in Ravana's court, who has been told by Ravana to stop you from fetching *Sanjivani* at any cost."

Kalanemi was surprised to find Hanuman return alive from the lake. Before he could speak a word, Hanuman caught him by his throat, snapped his neck and flung his corpse with such force that it landed up in Lanka in Ravana's court.

The Sun and the Moon

Fearing that Hanuman would fetch the *Sanjivani* in time to save Lakshmana, Ravana ordered the sun to rise and the moon to set before the appointed hour. Hanuman saw the moon slip rapidly towards the horizon and the first light of the dawn appearing beyond the hills. Divining Ravana's intentions, Hanuman rushed to the horizon, caught the moon between his jaws and trapped the sun in his armpit.

Time was running out. Hanuman feared that if he went around Gandhamadana searching for the herb, he would lose precious time. To expedite things, Hanuman decided to carry the entire hill to Lanka.

Hanuman grew in size till his head brushed against the sky. He then uprooted the hill, placed it on his palms and rushed south to Lanka.

Hanuman and the crocodile-nymph; Temple wall carving from Tamil Nadu

71

Hanuman traps the sun in his armpit as he rushes back with the mountain of herbs; illustration by author

Gods, demons, humans, birds, beasts, reptiles, fishes, all who saw Hanuman flying across the Jambudvipa and over the sea to Lanka, hill in hand, were awe-struck by his strength and agility.

Mandodari Kicks Ravana

When Hanuman arrived on the shores of Lanka and placed Gandhamadana on the ground, the monkeys roared joyously. Sushena scoured the slopes and found the *Sanjivani* herb. "Now all I need is the divine pestle and mortar that Ravana keeps in his inner chambers."

Hanuman immediately made his way into Ravana's palace. Unfortunately, Ravana had foreseen Sushena's need for the pestle and mortar and had placed it on a table next to his bed, determined not to let it out of his sight.

Hanuman noticed that Mandodari was sleeping soundly next to Ravana and came up with a plan to distract the *rakshasa*-king. He slipped under Ravana's bed and tied Ravana's hair to the bedpost. He then grabbed the pestle and mortar and ran towards the door.

Ravana tried to run after Hanuman but was yanked back to his bed because his hair that had been tied to the bedpost. He tried to untie the knot but failed because Hanuman had cast a spell: the knot would not be undone until Mandodari kicked Ravana on the head with her foot.

Hanuman jeered Ravana as the mighty Lord of Lanka woke his wife up, bowed his head and begged her to kick him. Hanuman then took to the air and gave Sushena the divine pestle and mortar.

Hanuman and the mountain of
herbs; Mysore painting

Lakshmana Saved

Using the pestle and mortar fetched from Ravana's palace, Sushena made a paste of *Sanjivani* and smeared it all over Lakshmana's body. Its medicinal essence seeped through Lakshmana's skin, entered his bloodstream and counteracted Indrajit's poison.

In no time Lakshmana regained his consciousness. He stood up, ready to do battle. "Bring me my bow. I can't wait to kill Indrajit."

Suddenly, Rama noticed that neither the sun nor the moon could be seen in the sky. "Where are they?" he asked.

"Oops," said Hanuman, opening his mouth to liberate the moon and raising his arms to liberate the sun. "I was forced to imprison them because Ravana had ordered the moon to set and the sun to rise before the appointed hour."

As the moon and the sun returned to their celestial abodes, Rama and Lakshmana embraced Hanuman unable to find words to express their gratitude.

Rama embraces Hanuman in gratitude; modern illustration

Disruption of Indrajit's Sacrifice

In the battle that followed, Lakshmana fought fiercely and worsted the *rakshasa* army, forcing Indrajit to take shelter behind the walls of Lanka.

Word reached Vibhishana that Indrajit planned to perform the *Abhichara* sacrifice that very night. "If he succeeds, he will become invisible and invulnerable," said Vibhishana. He led Lakshmana and Hanuman to a secret sacrificial ground on the southern shores of Trikuta. There, under the banyan tree, surrounded by a contingent of soldiers, they found Indrajit invoking fierce cosmic forces.

Hanuman disrupts Indrajit's sacrifice; Chitrakathi painting from Maharashtra

Hanuman pounced on the soldiers and drove them away enabling Lakshmana to shoot an arrow at Indrajit, forcing him to abandon his *yagna*, pick up his weapons and return to the battlefield, unprotected by the power of sacrifice.

Indrajit battles Hanuman; North Indian painting

After a great fight, Lakshmana's arrow severed Indrajit's neck. The warrior's head flew into the air and fell into Ravana's lap.

Mahiravana Joins Ravana

Shaken by Indrajit's death, Ravana sent for his other son Mahiravana, a powerful sorcerer who was ruler of Patala, the netherworld.

Mahiravana was a great devotee of the goddess Kali. He offered the goddess human sacrifices. In exchange, she revealed occult secrets of the universe.

Hanuman, holding a banner and leading the army of monkeys into battle; Ganjifa painting from Mysore

Like Kumbhakarna, Mahiravana did not want to fight Rama because he felt Rama's cause was just. But he changed his mind as soon as Ravana said, "Think of the powers the goddess Kali will grant you when you offer her the heads of two handsome and virile youths like Rama and Lakshmana."

Mahiravana Abducts Rama and Lakshmana

News of Mahiravana joining forces with Ravana alarmed Vibhishana. As a defence against Mahiravana's sorcery, he asked Hanuman to stretch his tail, wind it around Rama and Lakshmana and create an enclosure where the

Hanuman uses his tail to make a fence around Rama; Pahari painting

two brothers would be safe. Hanuman guarded the entrance while monkeys were deployed all around to keep watch.

At night, Mahiravana approached the monkey camp. To gain access into the enclosure, he cast a spell of sleep. All except Hanuman succumbed to the spell. Mahiravana then conjured up demons to breach the fence. But they were killed by Hanuman before they got a chance to even touch his tail.

Realizing that Hanuman was stronger, Mahiravana decided to use trickery to gain access into the enclosure. With his magical powers, he took the form of Vibhishana and approached Hanuman. "I want to see if the brothers are comfortable," he said. Hanuman failed to recognize the imposter and let him enter.

By the time Hanuman realized he had been duped, it was too late. The brothers were missing. In place of their bed was a tunnel stretching deep into the bowels of the earth, right down to Patala, the subterranean kingdom of Mahiravana.

Mahiravana abducts Rama and Lakshmana; Pahari painting

Hanuman's Son Makaradhvaja

While Vibhishana and the monkeys mourned the loss of Rama and Lakshmana, Hanuman dived into the tunnel and made his way to Patala, determined to rescue the brothers.

After a long journey, Hanuman reached Mahiravana's kingdom. At the gates, he was stopped by the doorkeeper who challenged him to a fight. The doorkeeper turned out to be quite a wrestler. Impressed, Hanuman enquired about his lineage.

"I am Makaradhvaja, the son of Hanuman," he said.

"Liar. I am Hanuman, Rama's devotee, sworn to celibacy. I have neither wife nor son."

Makaradhvaja fell at Hanuman's feet and revealed the secret of his birth, "As you flew across the ocean in search of Sita, a drop of your sweat fell into the sea. It was swallowed by a dolphin who as a result became pregnant and gave birth to me."

Makaradhvaja apologized for not recognizing his father and for engaging him in a duel. Hanuman embraced his son and showered blessings upon him.

Hanuman with his son Makaradhvaja; illustration by author

Hanuman Kills Mahiravana

On learning of his father's mission, Makaradhavaja led Hanuman to the Kali temple where Rama and Lakshmana were being held captive.

Hanuman found the brothers anointed with mustard oil, smeared with vermilion powder, bedecked with marigold flowers, ready to be sacrificed. Mahiravana was sharpening the sacrificial blade and chanting hymns to invoke the goddess.

When the goddess appeared, Hanuman took the form of a bee and asked her if she wanted Rama to die. "No," replied the goddess. "I would rather drink Mahiravana's blood."

With the blessings of Kali, Hanuman whispered into Rama's ear, "When Mahiravana asks you to place your neck on the sacrificial block, inform him that as a member of the royal family you have never learnt to bow your head. Tell him to show you how."

Rama did as he was told and demanded that Mahiravana demonstrate how a sacrificial victim is expected to place his neck on the altar. Exasperated, Mahiravana bowed his head in the ritually prescribed manner.

No sooner had Mahiravana done that then Hanuman seized the sacrificial blade and beheaded the sorcerer.

Hanuman beheads Mahiravana before the image of Kali; illustration by author

77

Hanuman returns triumphantly after rescuing Rama and Lakshmana from the kingdom of Mahiravana; Calendar art

The goddess Kali drank Mahiravana's blood. Satiated, she blessed Hanuman and recognised him as her attendant.

The residents of Patala were so impressed by Hanuman's actions that they begged Hanuman to stay back and be their king. "No, I go where Rama goes. In my place, I appoint Makaradhvaja as your king." The residents of Patala accepted Hanuman's decision.

After crowning Makaradhvaja king, Hanuman lifted Rama and Lakshmana on to his shoulders and flew back to earth, ready to resume the battle with Ravana.

Hanuman Liberates the Celestial Bodies

News of Mahiravana's fall filled Ravana's heart with fear. He consulted astrologers who looked into his horoscope and said, "The alignment of the celestial bodies is not in your favour."

"Maybe, I can change the alignment of the celestial bodies," thought Ravana. He mounted his flying chariot, rose to the skies, captured the nine celestial bodies, the *graha*s, and herded them to Lanka in chains. He then began a ritual that would force the *graha*s to realign themselves in his favour.

When Vibhishana learnt of this secret ceremony from his friends in Lanka, he immediately led Hanuman and a band of monkeys through a secret passage to the sacrificial hall of Ravana, intent on disrupting the ritual. They found Ravana sitting beside the fire-altar, his eyes shut, mouthing *mantra*s.

Led by Hanuman, the monkeys let out a piercing war-cry, rushed into the hall, blew out the sacred fire, kicked the ceremonial utensils and wiped off the occult diagrams painted on the floor. Unfortunately, none of this roused Ravana from his deep meditation. He continued chanting the magic formulas. "We must stop him at any cost," shouted Vibhishana, "Or he will succeed in changing the course of destiny."

Hanuman came up with a plan. He ordered his companions to frighten Ravana's wives. The monkeys rushed into the inner apartments of palace, alarming the women there. They attacked Ravana's queens and concubines, pulling their hair, scratching their faces, biting their fingers and tearing their clothes. "Help, help," they cried. Still Ravana did not open his eyes.

Hanuman and the monkeys then gathered around Mandodari. They bared their teeth, beat their chest and began to grunt menacingly. Terrified, Mandodari lamented, "Woe is me. My husband meditates while monkeys threaten my chastity."

Chandra, the moon-god, one of the nine celestial bodies that control fate; Pahari painting

Hanuman leaving the nether regions
with Rama on his shoulders and
with Mahiravana's head at his feet;
Thai painting

Mandodari's words shamed Ravana to open his eyes, terminate the ritual and rush to her defence. Having successfully distracted Ravana, Hanuman ran back in the sacrificial hall. He liberated the nine celestial bodies who returned to their celestial abodes to determine the fate of the *rakshasa*-king.

For having successfully destroyed Ravana's attempt to subvert fate, Hanuman won the eternal gratitude of the *graha*s.

Ravana's Queens

To protect their husband, Ravana's wives began performing a *vrata*, fasting and keeping all-night vigils, to rouse the forces of Nature in Ravana's defence.

Jambuvan knew that the *vrata* would come to naught if adulterous desires arose in the heart of Ravana's wives. He requested Hanuman to fly just above Ravana's palace.

From the palace window, Ravana's wives saw Hanuman — they admired his lithe limbs, his graceful movements, his upraised tail. For a brief moment, they wondered what it would be like to be his wife, to have his strong arms around them.

The mental infidelity of Ravana's wives sapped the *vrata*'s capacity to protect Ravana. Ravana was thus left vulnerable to the weapons of Rama.

Monkeys storm Ravana's palace; Mughal painting

Ravana enters the battlefield;
Mughal painting

Hanuman Silts the Lotus Lake

Ravana finally rode into the battlefield on a chariot drawn
by black stallions. He looked resplendent in his golden
coat of mail.

Rama, who had no chariot, faced him seated on
Hanuman's shoulders.

A great battle ensued. Ravana used his twenty arms
to rain missiles at Rama. Hanuman moved gracefully
on the battlefield dodging every weapon hurled by
Ravana so that not one of them scratched Rama's skin.

Rama managed to shoot an arrow that severed Ravana's
neck. To his surprise, the head grew back instantly.
This happened several times.

Frustrated, Rama sought Vibhishana's advice. "It is
rumoured that there is a pond in Ravana's garden into
which fell a drop of *amrita*, the nectar of immortality, a
long time ago." revealed Vibhishana. "Lotuses which
grow in this pond are imbued with the power to
regenerate the body and heal even the most lethal of
wounds. Ravana must be eating these lotuses every time
he is injured, thus saving himself."

That night, Hanuman took the form of bee, followed
Ravana into a garden where he found the rumoured lotus-
lake. Before Ravana could pluck a lotus, Hanuman moved
with lightening speed to swallow each and every lotus
and to silt the pond.

Ravana was thus deprived of the flowers that prevented
his fall in battle.

81

Mandodari and other queens
mourning Ravana's death; Mughal
painting

Final Battle

At dawn, the next day, Ravana offered prayers at his
Shiva temple and prepared to ride into the battlefield,
certain to meet his death.

Mandodari begged Ravana to let Sita go and make peace.
But Ravana was too arrogant to surrender. "When it is
time to fall, the mind does foolish things," Mandodari
realized as she bid her husband farewell.

The gods assembled in the skies to witness the final
battle between Rama and Ravana: Ravana on his chariot,
Rama on Hanuman's shoulders. The two warriors raised
their bow and shot lethal arrows at each other. It was a
fierce battle. Indra, king of the gods, offered his celestial
chariot to aid Rama during the course of the battle.

Finally, on Hanuman's suggestion, Rama decided to
shoot the *Rudrastra*, an arrow reverberating with the
power of Shiva. Advised by Vibhishana, he shot it into
Ravana's navel, the *rakshasa*-king's most vulnerable spot.

The arrow struck right on target and the *rakshasa*-king
tumbled down, his limbs numb, his breath shallow. It was
time for him to die.

Ravana's Wisdom

Mandodari rushed into the battlefield when she heard of
Ravana's fall. Her hair was unbound. Tears streamed
down her cheeks. She beat her breasts in sorrow and
threw herself upon Ravana's blood-stained body
lamenting his defeat and cursing her fate.

The *rakshasa*s mourned with their queen while the
monkeys celebrated their victory, cheering, clapping,
singing and dancing.

While everyone was busy rejoicing, Hanuman advised Rama, "Ravana was unrighteous in abducting Sita but let that not overshadow the fact that he is a great scholar, well versed in the scriptures. Take advantage of his immense knowledge before he dies."

Both Rama and Lakshmana went to the dying Ravana to learn from him.

Standing over Ravana's head, Lakshmana said, "I have heard you know a lot. Pass on your learning before you die. And who better to receive it than us, the victors." Ravana turned his head away in silence, angering Lakshmana who walked away in a huff.

Kneeling at Ravana's feet, Rama saluted the *rakshasa*-king and said, "Ravana, you know I have hurt you not out of malice but out of husbandly duty to save my wife. I respect you as a scholar. I would appreciate it if you share your knowledge with me so that it is not lost to the world after you are gone."

Rama's words and deeds pleased Ravana. "I accept you as my pupil, Rama, for you sat at my feet, saluted me and spoke with humility as any good student should. It will be an honour to share my knowledge with you. I rejected Lakshmana because he was rude and discourteous, unworthy of enlightenment."

To the astonishment of all those gathered on the battlefield, the dying Ravana, with his head on Mandodari's lap, revealed to his enemy Rama, who sat at his feet, the subtleties of philosophy, politics, economics, fine arts, dance, music, theatre and statecraft.

Thus, the villain became a teacher and the hero a student.

Rama learning from Ravana; illustration by author

Sita's trial by fire; modern painting by Jamini Roy

Sita's Test

Hanuman flew into Lanka and informed Sita of Rama's victory. Her joy knew no bounds. She wanted to rush out and throw herself into her husband's arms. "That would not be proper," said Trijata, the only *rakshasi* who had been Sita's friend during her period of confinement. "Let me bedeck you with the sixteen love-charms of a bride so that you appear to your husband as you did on your wedding night."

Sita prepared herself and followed Hanuman to the shores of Lanka where flanked by an army of bears and monkeys, she found her Rama looking resplendant with the scars of battle.

Sita smiled at her husband. Rama did not smile back. "How do I know that in the weeks you have spent in Ravana's pleasure-garden you have not been unfaithful to me?" asked Rama.

"If I have been chaste, fire will not harm me," replied Sita who ordered Hanuman to pile wood around her body and set it on fire. The *vanaras*, *bhalukas* and *rakshasas* even the gods and Rama's ancestors, watched the fire rise upto the heavens and Sita stand amidst the flames unhurt.

Her purity thus proven, Sita emerged — resplendent as a goddess — and took her side beside Rama as his lawfully wedded and eternally faithful wife.

Vibhishana's Coronation

Rama crowns Vibhishana king of Lanka; Mysore painting

84

After Ravana had been cremated and the period of mourning was over, Vibhishana was crowned king of Lanka in the ritually prescribed manner.

To make peace between the *vanaras* and the *rakshasas*, Hanuman suggested that Sugriva's son be given in marriage to Vibhishana's daughter. Every one liked the suggestion and the marriage was solemnised and blessed by Rama and Sita.

Rama then prepared to return to Ayodhya. Along with Sita, Lakshmana, he mounted Vibhishana's flying chariot — the *Pushpaka Vimana* — and prepared to make the long journey home.

Just as he was about to leave, Rama asked Hanuman how he would like to be thanked for his services. Hanuman replied, "My lord, let me spend the rest of my days in your service."

"So be it," said Rama. Hanuman boarded the flying chariot and followed Rama to Ayodhya.

Rama returning to Ayodhya with Sita and Lakshmana aboard Ravana's flying chariot; modern illustration

Traditional Location of some Sites in India (Jambudvipa) mentioned in the Ramayana

THAR
DESERT

● **AYODHYA**
(Dasharatha's Kingdom
in the land of KOSALA)

● **MITHILA**
(Janaka's Kingdom
in the land of VIDEHA)

VINDHYA MOUNTAINS

● **PANCHAVATI**
(from where Sita
was abducted)

DANDAKA
ARANYA

● **KISHKINDA**
(Sugriva's Kingdom)

● **RAMESHVARAM**
(where Hanuman met
Sampati)

● **LANKA**
(Ravana's Kingdom)

Hanuman in Ayodhya

Chapter IX

Hanuman Tests Bharata

After crossing the sea, the plains of Kishkinda, the Dandaka forest and the Vindhya mountains, the flying chariot entered Aryavarta. Soon it hovered over Kosala, Rama's homeland.

"Before I enter, I want to make sure that Bharata is parting with his crown willingly. Fourteen years is a long time and he may have changed his mind," said Rama.

On his orders, Hanuman paid a visit to Bharata disguised as a sage. He found Bharata and Shatrughna living as hermits in the village of Nandigrama on the outskirts of Ayodhya. He also found that Bharata had placed Rama's sandals on the throne and called himself his brother's regent.

"Why do you deprive yourself of kingship that your mother secured for you with her machinations? All is fair in politics. Don't feel guilty about taking the crown. All this talk of righteous civilised conduct is for weaklings and fools. Enjoy power, don't give it away," Hanuman told Bharata.

Bharata was not amused by what he heard. "Go away, you wicked sage. Your words have no effect on me. I, like Rama, am the upholder of *dharma* and I would rather die than sacrifice it on the altar of ambition."

Hanuman reported what had transpired between him and Bharata much to Rama's delight. The brothers met in Nandigrama. Everyone shed tears of joy.

Hanuman disguised as a sage talks to Bharata; Kutch wall painting

Urmila Wakes up

As soon as Rama and his retinue were on the outskirts of Ayodhya, Urmila woke up from her deep slumber.

Urmila was Lakshmana's wife. The goddess of sleep had promised Urmila that she would sleep for fourteen years while her husband was away. During this period, Lakshmana did not sleep at all so that he could serve his brother day and night.

After waking up, Urmila bedecked herself and gathered all the women of the royal household to prepare for a grand welcome.

The palace was decorated with wreaths of leaves and flowers. The floor was washed and polished. Incense was placed in the corners to drive out malefic spirits. Lamps were lit along passages. Sacred symbols were painted on doorways. Conches were blown. Flowers were showered

Urmila wakes up; Pahari painting

Rama enters Ayodhya after his long
exile; Mughal painting

on the road leading to the palace. Perfumed water was
sprinkled all around. Bright banners fluttered atop every
house.

The people cheered as Rama entered Ayodhya with
Sita by his side, followed by Lakshmana. Bharata and
Shatrughna also accompanied them.

The whole city rejoiced at the return of the sons of
Dasharatha.

Rama's Coronation

The *rakshasa*s led by Vibhishana, the *vanara*s led by
Sugriva, the *bhaluka*s led by Jambuvan, the vultures led by
Sampati and the sages led by Agastya, all made their way
North to attend the coronation of Rama.

88   Coronation of Rama; Modern
illustration

It was a grand affair. Bright pavilions were erected in the palace courtyard and a seat of gold was prepared where Rama would be crowned lord of Ayodhya.

Hanuman at Rama's feet during his coronation; Rajasthani painting

Dasharatha's three wives prepared Rama. They discarded his clothes of bark, undid his matter hair, and washed away every trace of forest life they found on his body. They anointed him with oil, sandal and turmeric paste, bathed him with milk, curd, butter and perfumed water, bedecked him in bright yellow silk, garlands of fragrant flowers and gem-studded ornaments of gold.

Sita was decorated with the sixteen love-charms of a bride.

When Rama sat on his throne, with Sita on his left lap, Bharata held the parasol, Lakshmana waved the fly-whisk, Shatrughna held the banner and Hanuman offered his hand as the footstool.

The crown of kings shone on Rama's head — it was the start of *Rama-rajya*, the rule of Rama, the era of perfection.

Rama and Sita Educate Hanuman

Hanuman lived in the royal palace with Rama and Sita, serving them dutifully. He would always be seen seated at their feet, listening to every word they spoke. Pleased with his devotion, the divine couple revealed to him the mysteries of life.

"I am *purusha*, the eternal infinite unchanging spirit, causation personified," said Rama.

89

Rama and Sita instructing Hanuman;
Bronze idol from Tamil Nadu

"I am *prakriti*, cosmic matter, embodiment of
manifestation. All things that exist have form because of
me. I am the cradle of Time and Space that holds all
things together," said Sita.

"Together we constitute the universe. We validate
each other's existence and delight in each other's
company."

Hanuman learnt that Rama was *paramatma*, the soul of the
universe. Sita was *Jivatma*, the soul of the individual.
Ravana who separated them was *ahankara*, the ego. He
who united them was *bhakti*, devotion.

Hanuman Tears Open his Chest

Sita gave Hanuman a necklace of pearls. With simian
curiosity, Hanuman broke the necklace and inspected each
and every pearl. "What are you looking for?" asked the
residents of Ayodhya.

"For Rama and Sita," replied Hanuman.

"They are seated on the throne."

"They exist in all things. I know they reside in my heart.
I am trying to find them in these pearls."

Hanuman's naiveté made everyone in Ayodhya laugh.
"So Rama and Sita reside in your heart, do they? Can you
show them to us," they teased.

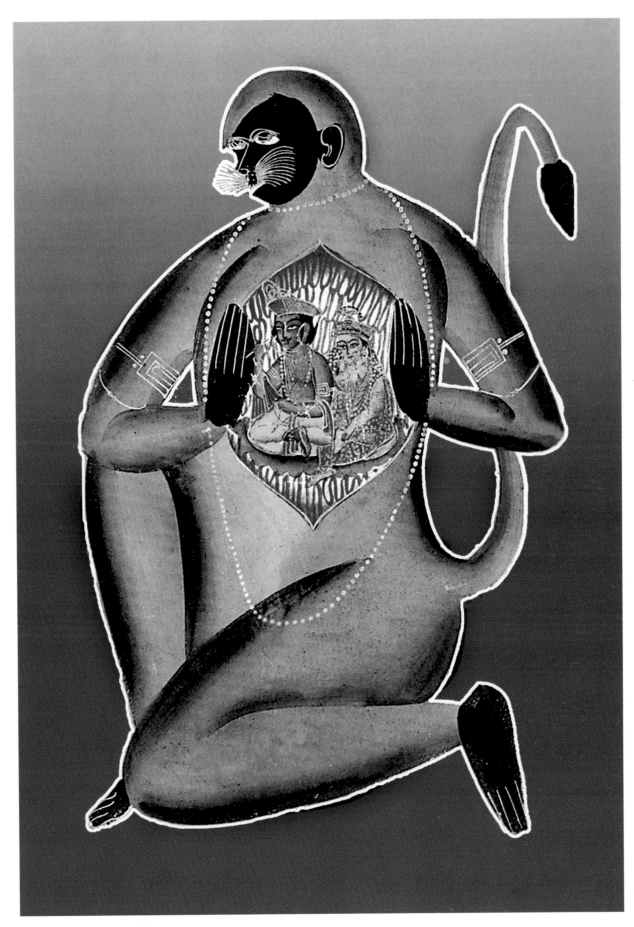

Rama and Sita in Hanuman's heart;
Kalighat painting from Bengal

Hanuman tears open his chest to reveal Rama and Sita; Calendar art

Hanuman immediately ripped open his chest with his sharp nails. There, within his chest, on his heart, the people of Ayodhya were astonished to find the image of Rama and Sita.

Never again did anyone make fun of Hanuman's devotion.

The Vermilion Dot

Every morning, Hanuman saw Sita paint a red dot on her forehead and smear the parting of her hair with vermilion powder. "Why do you do that?" he asked.

"For the good of Rama," replied Sita.

Hanuman also wanted to do something for the good of Rama. "If Sita has to paint a dot on her forehead to achieve this, an ordinary monkey like me must do something more," he thought. So he took vermilion powder and smeared his whole body with it.

Both Rama and Sita were moved by Hanuman's display of affection. Since that day Hanuman's images are painted red.

The Power of Rama's Name

Rama once picked up his bow to kill Kuvachana, a youth who had insulted his ancestors. To save himself, Kuvachana sought the protection of Hanuman. Without learning of the nature of his crime, Hanuman promised to defend Kuvachana at any cost.

When Hanuman saw Rama approach bow in hand, he realised he had been tricked into offering Kuvachana protection. Unable to go back on his word, he stood between Rama and Kuvachana.

Chanting the name of Rama, Hanuman created a protective enclosure around Kuvachana using his tail. The enclosure reverberated with the power of Rama's name. No matter how hard Rama tried, he could not breach this enclosure.

"More powerful than Rama is the name of Rama," declared Hanuman.

The gods intervened to end the stalemate. Rama was allowed to kill Kuvachana to avenge the insult to his ancestors. Hanuman was allowed to bring Kuvachana back to life with the power of Rama's name.

Doubts on Sita's Character

While the people of Ayodhya rejoiced at the reunion of the royal family, Ravana's sister Surpanaka slipped into

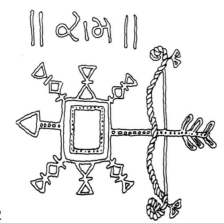

Sita with Surpanaka; illustration by author

Rama's palace disguised as a handmaiden determined to cause grief to Rama and avenge her brother's death.

She endeared herself to Sita and once, in a spirit of play, asked Sita how Ravana looked like. "I don't know. I never looked upon his face. I only saw his shadow cast on the sea on the way to Lanka." Surpanaka begged Sita to draw Ravana's shadow on the wall. Sita drew the outline innocently. While she was away, Surpanaka completed the picture and slipped out of the palace.

News of the painting of Ravana on the wall of Sita's inner apartments spread like wildfire. Doubts were cast on Sita's character. To add fuel to fire, Surpanaka asked the people of Ayodhya, "Whose child rests in Sita's womb, I wonder?"

Sita's Banishment

Hanuman went around Ayodhya determined to find the culprit.

Meanwhile, a washerman refused to let his wife into his house because she had taken shelter in another man's house for a night to escape from a storm. "I am no Rama to accept as my wife a woman who has spent a night with another man," he said.

Word of this incident reached Rama. He realised his people were unwilling to accept Sita as their queen. "Her soiled reputation stains the good name of the Raghava dynasty," they said.

By the time Hanuman returned to Ayodhya dragging Surpanaka by her plait, Rama had taken the decision to abandon Sita and uphold the honour of his family. Nothing would make him change his mind.

93

Hanuman watching over Sita and her sons; illustration by author

Sita Gives Birth to Luva and Kusha

When Sita expressed her desire to visit the forest where she had spent so many years during Rama's exile, Rama ordered Lakshmana to take her there. "Do not bring her back," he said.

In the forest, on learning of Rama's decision, Sita was distraught. At first she planned to kill herself, but the thought of Rama's children growing in her womb stopped her. Accepting the situation as her lot in life, she bid Lakshmana farewell and wandered deep into the woods where she found shelter in Valmiki's hermitage.

There, away from the whims of Rama's subjects, surrounded by birds and beasts, Sita gave birth to a pair of twins: Luva and Kusha. Confident in her chastity, she raised her sons single-handedly, teaching them the scriptures and the art of archery.

Rama meanwhile performed his stately duties placing a golden idol of Sita on the throne meant for queens. When his subjects requested that he remarry, he refused. "I have abandoned the woman you do not want as your queen, but I will forever remain faithful to the woman who is my wife," he said. Denying himself the privileges of a royal life, Rama lived in his palace like a hermit. Though deprived of all personal joy, he made sure that there was peace and prosperity in the lives of his subjects.

Hanuman followed Rama, serving him dutifully, not knowing how to reduce the burden of his master's grief.

Rama's Horse Sacrifice

Years later, Rama decided to perform the Ashwamedha *yagna*, a ritual that would make him *chakravarti* or universal emperor if successfully completed.

As part of the ceremonies, the royal horse was let loose and allowed to wander all over the earth. Every piece of land the horse traversed unchallenged came under Rama's sovereignty. Anyone who dared stop the horse had to stand up to the might of Rama's army.

Sita with her sons Luva and Kusha in Valmiki's hermitage; Pahari painting

94

Rama's youngest brother Shatrughna was put in charge of the soldiers following the royal horse. Rama ordered Hanuman to look after Shatrughna's wellbeing.

Hanuman seeking the medicinal herb that will save Shatrughna; Mughal miniature

Hanuman Saves Shatrughna

Rama's horse travelled to the four corners of the world. Most let the horse pass unhindered and became the vassals of Rama. The few kings who did try stopping the horse were successfully overpowered.

One king named Viramani tried to stop the horse from passing through his kingdom. He challenged Shatrughna to a duel. Though Shatrughna managed to defeat Viramani, he was seriously injured in the battle. An arrow had pierced his chest and the poison on the arrowhead spread through his body rendering him unconscious.

Luva and Kusha prepare for war; Rajasthani painting

Hanuman realised that Shatrughna would die unless he received an antidote. So he rushed to the slopes of the Himalayas in search of the *Sanjivani* herbs that had long ago saved Lakshmana's life. He found the medicinal plant, applied a paste of its leaves on Shatrughna's wound saving him just in time.

When Rama heard of this incident, he showered Hanuman with blessings.

Hanuman Captured

Some time later the royal horse of Ayodhya entered the forest where Sita had taken refuge. Her twins Luva and Kusha captured the horse and refused to part with it. "We refuse to accept the overlordship of a king who abandoned his pregnant wife," they said, raising their bows.

Luva and Kusha capture the royal horse of Ayodhya; North Indian miniature

A great war followed. The two boys withstood the might of Rama's army. They successfully managed to drive Shatrughna away. They even captured Hanuman, tied him to a post in their hut and treated him as an amusing pet.

When he could not untie himself, Hanuman realised the children who had captured him were none other than the sons of Rama. Accepting his situation, he began chanting the name of master. The chanting of Rama's name caught the attention of Sita who, unaware of these happenings, was horrified to find Hanuman imprisoned in her house.

Rama Meets his Sons

Rama, meanwhile, rode out of Ayodhya determined to teach the boys who had captured his horse a lesson.

Father and sons would surely have fought each had Hanuman not rushed between them. "Stop," he cried and introduced Rama to his sons. He explained, "Sita's righteous conduct has given her sons the

Luva and Kusha capture Hanuman; Chitrakathi painting from Maharashtra

power to defeat everyone who treated her unfairly.
Make peace for neither you nor any warrior of
Ayodhya can overpower these lads who have *dharma*
on their side."

Rama lowered his bow. So did Luva and Kusha, stunned
by the revelation. They rushed into each other's arms.
"My sons, my sons," cried Rama. Hanuman wept tears of
joy as he witnessed his master acknowledge his long
lost sons.

Rama returned to Ayodhya with his children.

Sita stayed back in the forest. The residents of Ayodhya
still did not accept her as their queen.

Sahasramukharavana

Meanwhile, a hundred-headed *rakshasa* called
Sahasramukharavana was causing havoc in Jambudvipa.

Sahasramukharavana was Ravana's son. He was but a
child when his father was killed. When he came of age, he
obtained from Brahma a boon that none but a truly chaste
woman would be able to harm him.

Fortified by this boon, he began harassing Vibhishana
in Lanka and Sugriva in Kishkinda. News of his
misdeeds reached Rama who prepared to do war against
this new foe.

Sahasramukharavana entered Kosala determined to
destroy Ayodhya. Neither Rama nor his armies could
stop his advance.

Sita and Hanuman attacking
Sahasramukharavana; illustration
by author

On learning of Brahma's boon, the women of Ayodhya were asked to enter the battlefield. Not one woman was chaste enough to defeat the dreaded *rakshasa*. Rama knew that there was only one woman who could save his city and his people — Sita.

Hanuman Fetches Sita

Rama feared that Sita would not come voluntarily to the city that had rejected her. So he made Hanuman tell Sita a lie, that he was dying. On hearing this, Sita rushed to Ayodhya to catch a glimpse of her husband before he passed away.

On the outskirts of the city, the *rakshasa* Sahasramukharavana blocked her path and refused to let her pass. Outraged by Sahasramukharavana's action, impatient to meet her dying husband, Sita picked up a blade of grass, transformed it into the lethal *Shaktika* missile with the power of her chastity and hurled it at the *rakshasa*. The missile ripped through Sahasramukharavana's heart and killed him instantly.

Rama and the residents of Ayodhya rushed out cheering Sita, their saviour.

When Sita saw Rama all hale and hearty, she realised the news delivered by Hanuman was a ploy to bring her to Ayodhya.

She told Hanuman, "In carrying out your orders, you uttered a lie that caused me to experience the horror of losing my husband. May you outlive Rama and know, in actuality, the pain of separation."

Sita Enters the Earth

Having witnessed in the killing of Sahasramukharavana the power of Sita's chastity, the people of Ayodhya were willing to welcome her back as their queen.

Looking at Rama and his subjects, Sita smiled wistfully and said, "There, the slanders have been stifled forever. My husband's honour and the dignity of his dynasty has been restored. My sons have found their father. I am needed no more. So if I have thought of none but Rama in my entire life, let the earth-goddess, who gave me to my father, take me back into her arms."

No sooner had Sita spoke these words than the earth shook. The ground beneath Sita split open and she disappeared into the earth. All Rama could do was watch helplessly. He embraced his sons and wept uncontrollably.

Rama spent the rest of his days beside the golden effigy of Sita, inconsolable in his grief.

Hanuman the formidable doorkeeper of Rama; temple sculpture

Rama's Ring

Not long after Sita's descent into the bowels of earth, the gods told Rama, "You have fulfilled your destiny on earth. Your time as a mortal has come to an end. You must return to Vaikuntha as Vishnu."

"So be it," said Rama.

"But Yama, the god of death cannot enter your palace because Hanuman guards your door. Send him away," requested the gods.

Accordingly, Rama dropped his signet ring in a hole in the ground.

"Please fetch it back," requested Rama. Hanuman dived into the hole in search of the ring.

The hole led Hanuman to *Naga-loka*, the land of serpents. There Hanuman found a huge platter full of rings, each one a perfect copy of Rama's signet ring.

The *naga*s who guarded the platter of rings told Hanuman, "There have been as many Ramas as there are rings on this plate. Every time the wheel of existence takes a turn, a Rama comes into being. Whenever an incarnation of Rama draws to a close his ring falls into the land of serpents. When you return to earth, you will find that Rama will be preparing to abandon his mortal body."

Yama, the god of death; Mysore painting

Banishment of Lakshmana

While Hanuman was away looking for the ring, a group of sages requested a private audience with Rama. Posting Lakshmana at the door of his private chambers with instructions not to let anyone in, Rama spoke to the sages.

While Rama and the sages were engaged in conversation, the short-tempered sage Durvasa demanded an audience with Rama. When Lakshmana tried to block his way the sage threatened to curse Ayodhya with a dreadful epidemic. To save Rama's subjects, Lakshmana let Durvasa enter.

For this act of disobedience, Lakshmana knew he could not show Rama his face ever again. He walked out of Ayodhya and into the river Sarayu, relinquishing his mortal body, having lost the will to live.

When Rama emerged from his private chambers to greet Durvasa, he found no trace of the sage. When he turned around, the sages inside had disappeared too. Lakshmana was not around either.

Rama realised he was all alone. It was time to leave the earth.

Rama Abandons the Earth

Rama embracing Hanuman;
calendar print

When Hanuman returned to earth after his visit to *Naga-loka*, he found the residents of Ayodhya, Bharata, Shatrughna, Luva, Kusha, Sugriva, Angada and Vibhishana lamenting on the banks of the Sarayu as Rama prepared to drown himself in the river and abandon his mortal body.

Rama had divided the kingdom of Kosala between his sons and had donated all his worldly possessions including his weapons, ornaments and clothes amongst the sages.

Having broken off all connections with the material world, Rama said, "Everything must come to an end. I have done my duty as Rama – upheld the laws of civilisation, obeyed my father, ruled my people and been faithful to my wife. Now it is time for me to leave earth."

"What about me?" asked Hanuman with tears in his eyes.

Embracing Hanuman, Rama said, "Live as the embodiment of devotion until people chant my name and remember my deeds. Join me when my name and my deeds are forgotten, for then civilisation will come to an end, anarchy will reign and *pralaya*, the flood of doom, will engulf the world."

Rama then submerged himself beneath the waters of the Sarayu, never to rise again.

Rama enters the river Sarayu to abandon his mortal body; illustration by author

Hanuman After Rama

Chapter X

Hanuman in the Himalayas

As foretold by Sita, Hanuman witnessed the departure of Rama from earth and experienced the heartbreak that followed.

As the years passed, he witnessed the deaths of all his friends and loved ones: Sugriva, Angada, Jambuvan, Vibhishana, Bharata, Shatrughna, Luva, Kusha. This was the price of being an immortal, a *chiranjeevi*.

All alone, Hanuman retired to the slopes of the Himalayas to experience *santana dharma*, the ultimate truth: "Rama is *purusha*, the eternal infinite unchanging spirit, causation personified; Sita is *prakriti*, cosmic matter, embodiment of manifestation. Together they constitute the universe."

He witnessed the unending transformations of matter — birth and death, joy and sorrow, aspiration and frustration, union and separation. In the flux of things, he felt the stillness of the soul, the serenity of Rama.

Inspired, he composed verses and made music in memory of Rama. His devotional songs, *bhajan*s and *kirtan*s, reverberated through groves, over hills, across valleys. Birds and beasts gathered around to watch Hanuman chant, without pausing for a breath, *Rama-nama*, the name of Rama.

Hanuman in a plantain grove chanting the sacred name of Rama; calendar art

Narada Hears Hanuman's Music

Both Narada and Tumburu played the lute or *vina*. Each one considered himself to be the best musician in the world. So they went to Vishnu to settle the dispute. Before giving his judgement, Vishnu asked them to hear Hanuman make music. The two agreed condescendingly and found the monkey on the icy slopes of the Himalayas.

"I am no musician," said Hanuman. "I only pluck the strings of my lute in the hope of capturing the glory of Rama." Picking up his *vina*, he began to sing. As the music filled the air, Narada and Tumburu were spellbound by the sheer passion in the melody and technical excellence of the sound.

Such was the power of Hanuman's music that the snow around started to melt. When the music stopped, the snow reformed. Narada and Tumburu realised they were stuck on the ice!

"Why don't you make music and make the snow melt once again so that you can free yourself?" suggested

Hanuman with his lute; illustration by author

101

Hanuman singing songs in memory of Rama; calendar art

Vishnu. But no matter how hard they tried, neither Narada nor Tumburu could make music that had the power to melt the ice.

Their melody lacked the divine power of Hanuman's composition. While theirs was the product of the ego, his was the product of a devoted heart.

Hanuman Reforms a Thief

A thief terrorised a forest path. In response to the plea of travellers, Hanuman took it upon himself to reform the thief.

"I murder and steal to support my family," the thief explained.

"Will your family share the punishment of your crimes?" asked Hanuman.

The thief questioned his family. While they were willing to survive on the loot he brought home, neither his wife nor his children were willing to share the punishment of his crimes.

"There you see," said Hanuman, "You and you alone are responsible for the deeds you do, irrespective of the motivation. You and you alone will reap the consequences of your actions."

Hearing this, the thief decided to abandon his criminal ways. "How do I wash away my sins?" he asked.

"Chant the name of Rama," replied Hanuman. Thief tried to chant, "Rama," but his tongue — condemned by years of crime — could not articulate the sacred name.

"Then chant — *mara, mara*," advised Hanuman. *Mara* means death; the thief's tongue could articulate this word with ease.

Hanuman raises his hand to reform wrong doers; temple wall carving from Tamil Nadu

102

The thief chanted, "Mara, mara...ma-ra, ma-ra...ma-ra-ma-ra-ma-ra-ma...ra-ma, ra-ma...rama, rama...Rama, Rama..." Thus the word meaning death reversed itself to form the name of Rama. While *mara* meant death, desire and delusion, Rama meant life, detachment and reality. The chanting of Rama's name washed away the sins of the thief and granted him enlightenment.

Bhima Tries Lifting Hanuman's Tail

Bhima, the mighty son of Pandu, was passing through a banana grove when he came upon an aged monkey lying across the road. "Get up and let me pass," he ordered the monkey.

"I am too old to get up. Walk around me, please," the monkey requested.

"You insignificant beast, you dare ask me to walk around you like a servant while you lie down like a king. Don't you know who I am? I am Bhima. Poets all over the world compose songs of my strength and valour. Demons tremble at the mention of my name. So get up and make way for me, before I kick you aside."

"I am ill and weak. Please, just brush my tail aside and pass."

Bhima decided to do just that. To his surprise, he found the monkey's tail too heavy to push. After several unsuccessful attempts, he decided to use his hand. First one, then both. He used all his strength, but the tail did not budge an inch. It was just too heavy.

Bhima realised this was no ordinary monkey. "Mighty monkey, tell me the truth. Who are you?"

The monkey identified itself as Hanuman.

Ashamed of his arrogance, Bhima fell at Hanuman's feet.

Bhima trying to lift Hanuman's tail; illustration by author

103

Arjuna's Bridge of Arrows

Arjuna, another son of Pandu, was the greatest archer in the world. Once, while walking along the seashore, he thought aloud, "Why, I wonder, did Rama use stones to build the bridge to Lanka? Why did he not make a bridge of arrows instead?"

"Because a bridge of arrows would not be able to bear the weight of even a single monkey," said Hanuman who happened to be passing by.

Arjuna did not accept Hanuman's argument. To settle the dispute he raised his bow and built a bridge of arrows across the sea.

Hanuman placed just one foot on this bridge and it collapsed. "There, what did I say."

Arjuna was so crestfallen at his failure that he decided to abandon archery altogether. At that moment, Krishna appeared on the scene . He asked Arjuna to build another bridge of arrows. "This time chant Rama's name while shooting every arrow."

Arjuna did as Krishna advised and the bridge did not collapse even when Hanuman jumped on it.

Krishna smiled. So did Hanuman. It dawned on Arjuna that it was not the material used that made the bridge to Lanka strong; it was the divine power of Rama's name that did the trick.

Hanuman in the Mahabharata War

The sons of Pandu, the Pandavas, lost their kingdom to their cousins, the Kauravas, in a game of dice. As per the wager, the Pandavas had to spend thirteen years in the forest before they could reclaim their kingdom. For thirteen years, the Pandavas lived in exile. In the fourteenth year, when they asked for their kingdom, the Kauravas went back on their word and turned them away. This led to the Mahabharata war on the plains of Kurukshetra.

Hanuman dancing on Arjuna's bridge of arrows; illustration by author

Hanuman residing in the banner
atop Arjuna's chariot; Calendar art

"Treat this, not as a war for a kingdom, but as a war of
righteousness," advised Krishna who supported the
Pandava cause. "Fight not with anger in your heart,
fight not for vengeance. Fight as the instrument of the
divine. Fight for justice with a clear mind and a
determined will."

Arjuna was appointed commander of the Pandava
forces. He requested Hanuman to serve as the insignia
on his banner. "You represent strength, intelligence,
wisdom and discipline that I need to bridle my passions
so that I can fight the battle as Krishna asks me to,"
said Arjuna.

Hanuman agreed and placed himself on Arjuna's banner.
The banner was mounted atop Arjuna's war-chariot and
it fluttered majestically as Arjuna led the Pandavas to
victory.

Hanuman Defends Vaishnavi

In the Treta *yuga*, the second quarter of the cycle of life,
Vaishnavi wanted to marry Rama but Rama turned her
request down because he was already married to Sita.
"I will marry you in Kali *yuga*, the final quarter of
the cycle of life," said Rama. So Vaishnavi decided to
live alone in the Himalayas as a mendicant until the
Kali *yuga* dawned.

One day, a sorcerer called Bhairo visited Vaishnavi.
Vaishnavi offered him food in keeping with the laws of
hospitality. Bhairo however was not interested in the
vegetarian food served before him. He wanted wine, meat
and also sexual union with Vaishnavi so that he could
perform an occult ritual.

Vaishnavi, who had sworn herself to Rama, refused to
indulge Bhairo. When he tried to use force, she ran away.
Bhairo ran after her.

For days, Vaishnavi ran over the hills trying to evade Bhairo but he kept pursuing her. Tired and thirsty, Vaishnavi sought Rama's help. At that moment, Hanuman appeared on the hills. He struck a rock with his foot to release a stream of fresh water. He punched a cave into the hillside.

While Vaishnavi drank the water and rested in the cave, Hanuman fought Bhairo. Vaishnavi stayed within the cave for nine months performing austerities. During this period Hanuman wrestled with Bhairo to keep him out.

Nine months later, shedding her human form, Vaishnavi emerged as Adi-Maya-Shakti, the supreme mother-goddess. She raised her trident and beheaded Bhairo.

She thanked Hanuman for his timely support and accepted him as her attendant and the eternal guardian of her shrine. From that day, the image of *langoor-vir,* the brave monkey, is placed on the gateway of any shrine built on the Himalayas dedicated to the mother-goddess.

Vaishnavi with Hanuman and Bhairava; calendar print

Hanuman and Matsyendranath

Matsyendranath wished to enter the shrine of Adi-Maya-Shakti and learn occult secrets from her. When Hanuman stopped him at the gate, there ensued a great fight between the two.

Hanuman found Matsyendranath to be a worthy opponent and let him in. Matsyendranath was so happy that he offered to do whatever Hanuman wished. "It is my wish that you go to *stri-rajya* and offer the women there the pleasure of your company," said Hanuman.

Stri-rajya was the land of women. The gods had decreed that any man who entered *stri-rajya* would die instantly. Hanuman discerned that only Matsyendranath had the power to withstand the curse of the gods.

Hanuman explained, "I promised the women of *stri-rajya* that I would provide them with the male companionship that they so desperately seek. You are the only one I have found capable of entering *stri-rajya* and pleasing them."

Matsyendranath went to *stri-rajya* and fulfilled Hanuman's wish.

Hanuman in the land of women; Phad painting from Gujarat

The Land of Women

Matsyendranath asked Hanuman what had made him promise male companionship to the women of *stri-rajya*. Hanuman narrated an event that had occurred long ago when he served Rama in Ayodhya:

Hanuman took care of Rama's every need much to the irritation of Sita. "You deny me the joy of serving my husband," she said. To keep him away from Rama, she hit upon an idea. "It is my wish that you father a child. Leave Ayodhya and return only when you have done so."

Sita's request horrified Hanuman. Prevented by his vow of celibacy from fathering a child, he feared he was doomed never to return to Ayodhya. In despair, he wandered the earth singing songs in memory of Rama.

The women of *stri-rajya* heard Hanuman sing. Such was the potency in Hanuman's voice that it made these women pregnant.

In due course they produced children who they presented to Hanuman. "Look, we have helped you father a child without breaking your vow of celibacy. Now you can return to the service of Rama."

Hanuman was so pleased that he offered the women a boon. "Send a man to *stri-rajya* for our pleasure," the women requested. Hanuman promised he would. Matsyendranath was the chosen man.

Matsyendranath, the great *Siddha-yogi*, calendar art

Hanuman writing the Ramayana on rocks; illustration by author

Valmiki Meets Hanuman

The sage Valmiki saw a hunter kill one of a happy pair of lovebirds. The female circled over her dead mate and cried over it. The scene so moved Valmiki that he cursed the hunter.

The curse, the sage realised, had taken the form of a poem — the rhythm of grief or *shoka* had inspired a verse or *shloka*, emotion or *bhava* had roused *rasa*, the essence of art. Following this aesthetic self-awareness, Valmiki proceeded to write the *Ramayana* to capture events and emotions in the separation and reunion of Rama and Sita.

Valmiki's poem became renowned in the three worlds as it touched the heart of every one who heard it.

One day, Valmiki heard that Hanuman had also written the story of Rama, engraving it with his nail on rocks. He travelled to the Himalayas to hear Hanuman's narrative.

When Hanuman read out his *Ramayana*, Valmiki was overwhelmed by the sheer power of the poetry. He experienced joy and sorrow. Joy, because it was so beautiful. Sorrow, because it overshadowed his own work.

When Hanuman saw the unhappiness his work had caused Valmiki, he set about smashing the engraved rocks. He did not want to take the credit away from the poet-sage. Such was the selflessness of Hanuman. For him writing Rama's story was the means to re-experience Rama, not the means to fame.

108

Hanuman represents different things to different people. Below are some of the ways he has been perceived through the ages.

Remover of Problems

Hanuman is known as *sankat-mochan*, he who gets rid of problems. In the *Ramayana*, Hanuman is always called upon to solve problems: he saves Sugriva from Vali's wrath and brokers a pact of mutual assistance between Sugriva and Rama. He finds Sita, oversees the building of the bridge to Lanka, brings the mountain of herbs that saves Lakshmana's life, destroys Indrajit's *yagna* and makes Ravana vulnerable to Rama's arrows.

Hanuman is the eternal enemy of demons who personify the problems in our life.

Patron of Physical Culture

Hanuman is closely associated with physical culture. His image is enshrined in gymnasiums all over the country. Gymnasts and wrestlers worship him before beginning exercise.

The *surya-namaskar*, salutation to the sun-god, is a simple mixture of exercise and ritual obeisance that was composed by Hanuman in honour of his celestial guru Surya. The exercise involves concentration, a full body stretch and push-ups.

Vayu, the wind-god, taught Hanuman *pranayama*. He in turn taught it to mankind. *Pranayama* or breath-control exercises build stamina and help discipline the mind.

Hanuman saluting the sun-god; illustration by author

109

Destroyer of Baneful Astrological Influences

In many images, Hanuman is shown trampling a woman and holding her by her plait. The woman embodies *panvati*, baneful astrological influences.

Hanuman has power over the *nava-graha*s, the nine celestial bodies whose alignment decides the fate of man. The nine *graha*s mentioned in *Jyotisha-shastra*, the Hindu science of astrology, are: *Ravi*, the sun; *Soma*, the moon; *Mangal*, Mars; *Buddha*, Mercury; *Brihaspati*, Jupiter; *Shukra*, Venus; *Shani*, Saturn; the bodiless *Rahu* and the headless *Ketu*.

The scriptures refer to several events where Hanuman exhibited his power over the celestial bodies. As a child, he mistook the rising sun for a fruit and tried to eat it. While carrying the mountain of herbs to save Lakshmana, he trapped the moon between his jaws and the sun in his armpit because he was told the herbs should be delivered before the sun rose and the moon set.

Hanuman overpowering *panvati*; idol from Gujarat

JUPITER SUN MOON VENUS MERCURY MARS SATURN RAHU KETU

110 Hanuman and the nine celestial bodies; illustration by author

Hanuman overpowering malevolent spirits; Tantrik painting

Guardian Against Sorcery

Sorcerers manipulate cosmic powers to invoke malevolent spirits. Hanuman is called upon to protect the world from such actions. When Ravana invoked two such spirits – Ahiravana and Mahiravana – to abduct and kill Rama, Hanuman turned the tables and sacrificed the two demons to the goddess Kali instead. Impressed, the goddess made Hanuman her doorkeeper who devotees could invoke to fight sorcery.

Hanuman is worshipped by Tantrikas who visualize him as a *mahasiddha*, master of occult powers. His ability to fly and to change his size and shape is believed to be the result of *siddhi*, power acquired through *brahmacharya* (total control over all biological urges).

Healer

Hanuman is associated with the healing arts or *Ayurveda* because he played a vital role in saving Lakshmana's life. He slipped into Lanka under cover of darkness to fetch the *rakshasa*-physician Sushena. He brought the mountain of herbs on time. He even managed to steal the magic pestle and mortar from Ravana's inner chambers to make the antidote.

After his return to Ayodhya, he also saved Shatrughna's life when he was wounded in battle.

Hanuman holding the mountain of herbs; modern sculpture

111

Hanuman, the *mahasiddha*; wood carving from North India

Soldier

Hanuman is a skilled warrior who uses both strength and guile to overpower the enemy.

He does not kill randomly. He spares Vali when the latter promises not to harm Sugriva. When the situation demands he does not shy away from violence. He kills Simhika, the sea-dragon, when she tries to eat him.

He does not succumb to false propaganda. When Indrajit kills a woman who appears to be Sita, Hanuman calls the bluff by turning into a bee and flying into Ravana's pleasure-garden where he finds the real Sita safe and sound.

He shows concern for the opponent, and fulfils Kumbhakarna's dying wish that his kinsmen should not see his body mutilated by monkeys.

Diplomat

In the *Ramayana*, the role of Hanuman as a skilled negotiator and shrewd diplomat is constantly stressed. He serves as envoy to both Sugriva and Rama.

Sugriva sends Hanuman to identify and befriend the strangers in the forest who turn out to be Rama and

Hanuman, the diplomat; Bronze image from Tamil Nadu

Lakshmana. Hanuman wins their confidence by his gentlemanly disposition and chaste use of language. Sugriva also sends Hanuman to pacify Lakshmana who loses his temper when he learns that Sugriva is unwilling to organise a search party at the end of the rainy season.

It is Hanuman who is sent by Rama to fetch Sita, twice: the first time from Ravana's pleasure-garden and the next time to defend Ayodhya against the *rakshasa* Sahasramukharavana. On his return from exile, Rama sends Hanuman to Ayodhya to find out if Bharata's really intends to give up the throne.

Hanuman the musician; folk-art from Gujarat

Musician

After the death of Rama, Hanuman retired to the slopes of the Himalayas where he spent his time making music in praise of Rama. He played the *vina* or lute and composed poetry in the memory of his divine master.

Hanuman was the first devotee to sing *bhajan*s, songs of adoration, and *kirtan*s, songs of praise.

His compositions are the product of devotion. They are not the creations of the ego. The sheer power of his music can melt rocks.

Scholar

Hanuman impressed both Rama and Ravana with his mastery over language, his grammar, his ability to use the right word in the right context and his perfect diction.

Hanuman playing the lute; illustration by author

113

He was the first poet to write the *Ramayana*. Such was the power of the poetry that it overshadowed the work of Valmiki.

Student

Hanuman represents the perfect student – humble, focussed, hardworking, determined and brilliant.

Hanuman was so determined to be the sun-god's student that he flew before the solar chariot as it made its way across the sky, withstanding the intense glare of the sun, listening to every word spoken by Surya.

Though highly educated, Hanuman never flaunts his knowledge. Instead, he sits at Rama's feet and continues the learning process.

Hanuman learning from Rama; South Indian wood carving

Hermit

Hanuman desires no fame or fortune. He lives – not in a palace or celestial paradise – but in mountains and groves.

He lives as a hermit, practicing *brahmacharya*, never indulging his senses. Celibacy is the highest manifestation of this discipline. It gives Hanuman's body so much power that his sweat makes a fish pregnant. His voice has the same effect on the women of *stri-rajya*.

Yogi

Yoga is the ability to control the mind. Hanuman is the perfect *yogi* with a disciplined mind.

He is a *gyan yogi* having controlled his mind through intellectual introspection and discernment. He learns about life from Rama and Sita, who personify the spiritual and material halves of the universe.

He is a *bhakti yogi* having controlled his mind through absolute faith in the divine. For him, every event in his life is *prasada*, the gift of the lord, to be experienced without question.

He is a *karma yogi* having controlled his mind through detached action. Hanuman served his master humbly, performing his duty without an eye on the rewards. His actions were never motivated by the desire for fame or fortune.

He is a *hatha yogi* having controlled his mind by the practice of *pranayama* or breath control and *asanas* or complex bodily postures to strengthen nerves.

He is a *laya yogi* with the knowledge to control his mind with chants (*mantras*) and charms (*yantras*). Thus, he has acquired *mahasiddha*, sacred occult powers.

114   Hanuman, the obedient servant; brass idol from Karnataka

Servant

Hanuman spends his entire life in the service of others. First, Sugriva, then Rama and finally, the mother-goddess. He performs his duty humbly and with devotion. He chooses not to marry and have a family so that he can submit himself totally to service.

He does whatever he is asked to do, even though he is often asked to do much less than what he is capable of. When he visits Lanka, he knows he can kill Ravana and rescue Sita on his own but he resists the temptation and does only what Rama has told him to do: find out Sita's whereabouts and establish contact with her.

Monkey

Despite his many ennobling qualities, Hanuman never renounces his simian nature. Like a monkey, he is restless, curious and mischievous, delighting all with his pranks. This is highlighted in Cambodian theatre.

Hanuman saluting Rama; Brass image from Maharashtra

Hanuman, the divine monkey seated on a pedestal created using his coiled tail; illustration by author

115

Hanuman carves the name of Rama on rocks he uses to build the bridge to Lanka; illustration from Gujarat

His restlessness leads him to destroy Ravana's pleasure-garden, the *Ashok-vatika*. His curiosity makes him search for Rama in the pearls that Sita gifts him. His mischief makes him tie Ravava's hair to his wife's plait when he enters Lanka in search of the magical pestle and mortar.

In *Ananda Ramayana*, the story goes that when the *rakshasa*s were trying to set his tail on fire, Hanuman repeatedly elongated his tail, shook the tip vigorously and put out the flames. The exasperated *rakshasa*s had to light the fire so many times that ultimately there was no oil left in Lanka; the golden city was plunged in darkness. To stir the flames, Ravana blew on the smouldering tail with his ten heads. The flames leapt up instantly, burning off Ravana's moustache, symbol of virility. Rejoicing over Ravana's humiliation, Hanuman jumped up and down and set Lanka ablaze.

Devotee

Hanuman is the embodiment of devotion. A temple dedicated to Rama is incomplete unless the image of Hanuman saluting Rama is placed facing the shrine. In North India, when the *Ramayana* is read out, a seat is kept vacant for Hanuman because it is believed that the monkey-god makes an appearance at every reading of the great epic.

The *Brihad-bhagavat-amrita* states that the sage Narada once asked Brahma who is the greatest devotee of Vishnu. Brahma, the creator of all things, directed him to Indra, king of the gods, who in turn directed him to Prahalada, king of demons. Prahalada pointed out Hanuman who chanted the name of Rama without a pause.

Hanuman saluting Rama and Sita; modern illustration

Attributes of Hanuman   Chapter XII

Physical Characteristics

Is the monkey-god of Hindus the red-faced *bandar* or the black-faced *langoor*? It is not clear. Some texts describe Hanuman as a golden monkey with a red face. Others state that after Hanuman had set Lanka on fire, he smothered the fire on his tail with his hands and then wiped his face. The soot on his hand made his red face black. In Thailand his bodyhair is said to be tipped with diamonds.

His shoulders are broad and strong. Often Rama and Lakshmana can be seen sitting on them. When Rama was fighting Ravana, he had no chariot so he sat on Hanuman's shoulder and rode into battle.

When Hanuman tore open his chest, Lakshmana found the image of Rama and Sita embedded in his heart.

Hanuman is depicted holding a mace in one hand and a mountain in the other, thus demonstrating his strength. Sometimes, his hand is extended as if he is about slap someone. Hanuman slapped Ravana when he spoke disrespectfully about Rama. Hanuman thus warns all creatures not to speak disrespectfully about Rama. The gesture doubles up as a sign of blessing and reassurance known as *abhaya mudra*.

Hanuman with upraised arm; amulet from Karnataka

Many-headed Hanuman

In his *virata-rupa* or awe-inspiring gigantic form, Hanuman is so tall that the stars in the sky serve as his diadem. In this form, he sometimes has five heads (*pancha-mukhi*) or eleven heads (*ekadasha-mukhi*) with ten or twenty hands.

In his *pancha-mukhi* form, the other four heads of Hanuman is sometimes that of horse, eagle, lion and boar representing Hayagriva, Garuda, Narasimha and Varaha, which are manifestations of Vishnu.

Tail

Hanuman's tail is arched upwards and is the symbol of strength, agility and virility. The tail can be lengthened and wound around.

Hanuman often uses his prehensile tail as a tool in his many adventures. He used it to create a throne for himself in Ravana's court. When Ravana set his tail on fire, he spun it around until every house in Lanka caught fire. Hanuman used his tail to whip up the sea to stun the fish who, under Ravana's instructions, were trying to destroy

Five headed Hanuman with tail arched upwards; calendar print

117

Rare image of Hanuman with eleven heads; sculpture from Varanasi

the bridge to Lanka. To protect Rama and Lakshmana from Mahiravana's sorcery, Hanuman coiled his tail around them and created a fortress.

Colour

Hanuman's idols are often smeared completely with *kumkum* or vermilion powder. Vermilion is a fertility colour and women paint a red dot on their forehead for the good for their husbands. It is said that when Sita told Hanuman that she put the *kumkum* on her forehead to express her love for Rama as his wife, Hanuman decided to smear his whole body with the powder to express his love for Rama as his devotee.

Hanuman is also smeared with saffron colour paste. Saffron is the colour of *brahmacharya* or continence. It is the colour of renunciation. He who wears this colour aspires to control his senses and overpower his ego so that he can gain enlightenment and get in touch with the divine. Hanuman is the perfect *brahmachari*: he never looks at women, he never seeks fame or fortune, he does not seek to gratify the flesh or indulge his ego.

Clothing

Hanuman wears earring made of five metals — gold, silver, copper, iron and tin. When he was in his mother's womb, Vali threw a missile of five metals to harm him. Such was the power of Hanuman that the missile melted the moment it touched his body and transformed into earrings.

Hanuman wears a loincloth, the standard garment of bodybuilders, wrestlers and gymnasts. It is said he was born with this loincloth or *kaupina* and it a symbol of his chastity. Hanuman does not threaten the world with his virility, as other warrior-gods do, and hence has earned the appreciation of the mother-goddess.

Round his neck, Hanuman has a necklace of pearls given to him by Sita. Hanuman searched every pearl looking for Rama, realizing ultimately that Rama rests not in external objects but in his heart.

Hanuman paints the mark of Vishnu on his forehead comprising of three vertical lines, the central using vermilion powder or *kumkum* and the other two using sandal paste.

Weapons

Hanuman is often shown holding a mace or club known as *gada*. This is both a weapon as well as a tool for bodybuilding used like dumbbells by Indian wrestlers.

Hanuman dancing on a demon with many weapons in his hands; sculpture from Nepal

In his five-headed form, he bears many more weapons such as a sword, a spear, a trident, an axe, a shield and a discus.

He sometimes is shown holding a boulder or a tree, associating him with primitive tribes and animals.

He also holds Rama's banner as he leads Rama's army into battle.

Demons Under Foot

Hanuman is often shown crushing a demon under his foot. This demon is variously identified as Ravana, Kumbhakarna, Indrajit, Kalanemi and Mahiravana.

Sometimes, Hanuman is shown trampling a woman. This woman represents *panvati*, baneful astrological influence. It also may be seen as Surpankha, Ravana's sister, who represents unbridled lust.

Hanuman holding Rama's banner; tribal art from central India

Hanuman trampling a male (left) and female (right) demon; images from Gujarat

Hanuman's strength displayed
as he holds mace in one hand and a
120   mountain in another; calendar art

Worship of Hanuman

Chapter XIII

Hanuman is worshipped for many reasons. Body builders, wrestlers and gymnasts worship him for strength and agility. Scholars and artists worship him because he is the patron of literature, grammar and music. He personifies discipline and devotion, power and modesty. He is *sankat-mochan*, the destroyer of problems. His help is especially sought to remove baneful astrological influences over which no man has control.

Shrines

Hanuman's images are usually enshrined on the frontiers of human settlements to keep out malevolent forest spirits, at crossroads where ghosts lurk, at the entrance of forts, palaces, temples and monasteries, in gymnasiums, on the gateway of Durga temples and before the shrine of Rama. In Puri, Orissa, it is said that Hanuman guards the four gates of the temple complex preventing the sound of the sea from entering the shrine and disturbing his master Lord Jagannath.

Hanuman in a yogic posture; temple image from Kerala

Hanuman's shrines, in keeping with his personality, are rarely elaborate. They are humble structures built by commoners without the intervention of priests. Hanuman is often seen in the open, under a tree, on the walls of a temple, fort or palace and on the roadside.

Idol

Hanuman statues are carved in stone or made using metal or alloys of gold, silver, copper, iron and tin. Sometimes the images are nothing but stones or stumps of trees with contours that vaguely resemble the monkey-god. These are covered with red paint or saffron paste and decorated with silver foil.

The image may either show Hanuman saluting Rama or standing guard or displaying his strength as he holds the mountain in one hand and his mace in the other. Rarely, the image may show Hanuman in a meditative posture like a *yogi* or holding a palm leaf like a learned scholar or resting a *vina* on his shoulder like a skilled musician.

Sacred Day

Hanuman is typically worshipped on Saturdays and Tuesdays, days that are associated with *Shani* and *Mangal* – Saturn and Mars, the two celestial bodies associated with death and war and known to disrupt human life with their influence.

Hanuman saluting Rama; temple image from Tamil Nadu

Hanuman with a garland of Calotropis gigantica leaves offered by devotees

Mysterious photograph clicked in 1999 shows a monkey with a Vaishnava mark on his forehead reading a scripture. Many believe this is Hanuman in reality.

Offering

Hanuman is offered *sindoor* (red lead), *til* (sesame) oil, husked black gram or *urad dal* (*Phaseolus radiatus*) and garlands of *Arka* (*Calotropis gigantica*) leaves and flowers. In South India, he is also offered butter and a garland of *vada*s (fried rice balls), his favourite food.

The red colour is the colour of strength and virility. The oil is the standard oil used by wrestlers, bodybuilders and gymnasts to massage their body. Clarified butter and *urad dal* are rich sources of protein that are consumed to generate energy, build strength, stamina and muscle mass.

The leaves and flowers offered to Hanuman grow in the wild and have medicinal properties. These befit his ascetic lifestyle.

Hymn

To invoke the powers of Hanuman, devotees read the *Sundara-kanda* of *Ramayana*, the chapter describing how Hanuman discovered Sita's whereabouts in Lanka.

Also popular amongst devotees is the *Hanuman Chalisa*, forty verses in praise of Hanuman, written by Tulsidas. It is said that the poet composed these verses when he was imprisoned in Fatehpur Sikri by the Mughal emperor Akbar. He chanted these verses for forty days at the end of which a vast army of monkeys gathered around Fatehpur Sikri and began destroying everything around. Akbar realised his folly and let Tulsidas go with honour. The monkeys left as soon as Tulsidas was released.

Festival

Anjani gave birth to Hanuman on the full moon day of *Chaitra* (March-April). On this day, known as *Hanuman Jayanti*, images of Hanuman are anointed with oil, decorated with sacred leaves and the *Ramayana* narrated in his presence for his pleasure.

Before Rama left the earth he offered Hanuman a boon in recognition of his selfless service. Hanuman asked that he live as long as man read the *Ramayana*. So to invoke the power of Hanuman, the *Ramayana* is read aloud regularly in temples and in homes on his birthday. During the recitation, a seat is prepared and kept vacant for Hanuman.

Relevance of Hanuman Today

Every Tuesday in Delhi and every Saturday in Mumbai, a long queue of men and women is seen outside Hanuman temples. They pour oil over the monkey-god's image, offer him a garland of leaves and salute him. Some sit around the shrine and chant the *Hanuman Chalisa*. Ask them why they do it, and you will get many answers: "Hanuman gives me strength to face my problems." "Hanuman will destroy those negative astrological influences that are making my life miserable." "I believe that by invoking Hanuman I will get what my heart desires." "Hanuman helped Lord Rama; he will also help me."

Imagine worshipping a monkey! Some may call this practice primitive superstition. Others, pagan practices with no modern-day relevance. Yet, for millions of Hindus, Hanuman embodies some of the most sublime values and philosophical ideas.

Let us try and understand what makes Hanuman such a popular and revered divinity.

Five-headed Hanuman; calendar art

Monkey and the Mind

In Hindu symbolism, the monkey represents the mind. Like a monkey, the mind is never still. If there is no work to be done, both are up to some mischief.

This monkey-mind happens to be the only thing over which man has absolute control. We cannot control the world around us, but we can control our mind. We cannot choose our life, but we can choose the way we respond to it.

According to ancient Hindu seers, there is no objective world 'out there'. The whole world is a subjective phenomenon, created by us. Our five senses (ears, eyes, nose, tongue and skin) capture data from the outside world. Our mind processes this data to create a bank of observations and opinions. This processing of data depends on the way the mind has been programmed.

Hanuman at Rama's coronation; calendar art

We – as humans – have the unique ability to programme and reprogramme our mind. In other words, we have the power to change the way we perceive life. And by changing our perceptions of life, we have the power of changing our world.

When Hanuman enters Rama's life, he changes Rama's world. He transforms a crisis (the loss of Sita) into an opportunity (rid the world of Ravana). He transforms a victim into a hero.

Hanuman; print from Gujarat

Thus, Hanuman is no ordinary monkey. He is the perfect mind. He embodies the highest potential that our mind can reach.

Strength

According to Yoga, the body is an extension of the mind. Hence, Hanuman — as the embodiment of the most evolved mind — has the most developed body. It is so strong that it can be used to lift mountains. It is so agile that it can be used to leap across the sea. Hanuman is *Vajra-anga-bali* or *Bajrang-bali*, he whose body is like thunder and whose movements are like lightning.

We do not believe that our mind is capable of such wonderful acts. Even Hanuman did not believe he had the strength to fly across to Lanka. He experienced a moment of self-doubt before he leapt from the peak of Mount Mahendra. But then, through faith, he discovered his miraculous strength. Had he remained trapped in doubt, he probably would have never crossed the sea and helped unite Rama and Sita.

Hanuman's image reminds us to seek the thunder and lightning within us.

Curiosity

The perfect mind is curious. Curiosity helps the mind discover talents. Hence, Hanuman discovered that he was not just a warrior but also a musician and a writer. His music melts ice and puts celestial musicians to shame. His poetry outshines the work of Valmiki, the lord of all poets.

Though talented, Hanuman is not complacent. He is eternally eager to learn more about the world. Hanuman was so determined to learn that he was not satisfied with any ordinary teacher. He wanted to learn from the sun-god himself, because the sun sees everything.

Curiosity helps the mind to learn more about itself and move towards perfection. Had Hanuman not been curious, he would not have found Rama and he would have remained just an ordinary monkey in Kishkinda with little chance of becoming a hero or a god.

The story of Hanuman goads us to be curious about ourselves and discover talents hitherto unknown.

Intelligence

The perfect mind is also intelligent. Hanuman's intelligence manifests in many ways. He is an excellent communicator, a shrewd diplomat and a clever trickster. He uses both his brawn and brain to succeed in his tasks.

Hanuman; clay-puppet from Andhra Pradesh

The intelligent mind knows that it possesses intellect (the capacity to judge the quality of information) and that it is fettered by the ego (that which separates oneself from the world around).

Intelligence uses the intellect to transform data into information and information into knowledge. Intelligence prevents the ego from overpowering the mind, so that knowledge transforms into wisdom.

Hanuman is both knowledgeable and wise. His personality exhorts us to be aware of how our mind works.

Selflessness

Selflessness is the measure of knowledge. The more we know, the more we realize that everything in life is impermanent, that nothing belongs to anybody and that any attempt to possess anything is bound to fail.

In the entire *Ramayana*, Hanuman does nothing for himself. All his feats are performed in the service of others. When Hanuman narrated the *Ramayana* to his mother Anjani, his mother asked, "Why did you not kill Ravana yourself? You could have done so with a flick of your tail and become more famous than Rama." To this Hanuman replied, "My life was not about winning fame for myself. It was about serving Rama."

His greatest act of selflessness comes to light when he destroys his version of the *Ramayana* so that his work does not overshadow that of Valmiki. His actions make us ask ourselves: for whom do we live our life?

Five headed Hanuman sitting on a crocodile; Kangra painting

Indra trying to prevent Hanuman from gobbling Surya, the sun-god; illustration by author

Hanuman meditating before a copy of the *Ramayana*; calendar art

Humility

Humility is the measure of wisdom. The wise man knows that discrimination is the result of delusion. Good and bad, right and wrong, greatness and smallness are matters of opinion and based on artificial standards. Hence, Hanuman is proud of nothing.

Here is a god who can gobble up the sun, who can leap into the sky with a mountain in one hand, who changes his shape and size at whim. Yet, he is content to stand as a doorkeeper in the temple of Rama and Durga. He makes no attempt to assert his greatness. Hanuman's humility mocks human arrogance. It forces us to ask ourselves: why do we publicize our achievements? why do we think they make us special?

Discipline

Sex and violence are natural urges. In animals, these urges are ruled by instinct. In humans, they are governed by choice. We can choose to live an unbridled existence, doing whatever makes our ego happy; or we can tame the beast within us.

The perfect mind tames the natural urges perfectly. Hence, Hanuman is a *param-brahmachari*. He neither indulges his senses nor inflates his ego. He has full control over his body and does not succumb to desire or ambition. He is celibate and chaste, in mind and body.

Like Hanuman, Ravana is strong, intelligent, and talented, But he is neither humble nor selfless. He is lustful and brutal. That is because he has succumbed to the ego. When man indulges the ego, he loses touch with the divine. So while Ravana is the Rama's enemy, Hanuman is Rama's friend.

The question Hanuman places before us: Is our life governed by our ego or are we moving towards the divine?

Devotion

To overpower the ego, to control the urges of sex and violence, and to realize the divine, Hindu scriptures strongly recommend *bhakti*, total submission to the will of the divine.

Hanuman personifies *bhakti* or devotion expressed through *dasya bhava*, the emotion of servitude. Devotion is the ultimate weapon to destroy the ego (Ravana) and to unite our soul (Sita) with the divine (Rama). We have to follow his path, if we seek *moksha* or liberation from earthly woes.

As the embodiment of *bhakti*, Hanuman is portrayed as a celibate *brahmachari* (sexual urge under control), who fights only for the good of others (violent urges under control) as he serves his master humbly and selflessly (ego under control).

A prayer to Hanuman is a prayer in our struggle to overpower the beast within us.

Though animal, Hanuman succeeds where most humans fail, hence he has been given the status of god. In Hanuman, we find the perfect example of devotion, discipline, humility, selflessness, intelligence, talent and strength. He is what our mind can potentially be.

Jai Hanuman

जय हनुमान

Victory to the mighty monkey-god

Hanuman Chalisa

This hymn of forty verses that glorifies Hanuman was written by Tulsidas, a 16th century poet-saint. It is said to bring into the devotee's life peace, affluence, strength, fearlessness, ecstasy, equanimity, bliss and ultimately, liberation from worldly things.

DOHA

> *Shri guru charan saroj raj*
> *Nij manu mukuru sudhari*
> *Varnau Raghuvar vimal jasu*
> *Jo dayaku phal chari*

Having cleansed my mind with the dust of my Guru's feet, I salute Rama, bestower of the four goals of life (righteous conduct, economic activities, pleasurable pursuits, spiritual practices).

> *Buddhihin tanu janike*
> *Sumirau Pavan Kumar*
> *Bal budhi vidya dehu mohin*
> *Harahu kalesa vikar*

Knowing that I am devoid of intelligence, I focus my mind on the son of the wind-god and ask for strength, intelligence, knowledge to relieve me of all that causes pain and suffering.

Hanuman tearing open his chest to show Rama and Sita; calendar art

CHAUPAI

1. *Jai Hanuman gyan gun sagar*
   Jai Kapis tihun lok ujagar

   Salutations to Hanuman, the ocean of wisdom and virtue, Salutations to the monkey-god whose glory illuminates the three worlds.

2. *Ram doot atulit bal dhama*
   Anjani-putra Pavansut nama

   The servant of Rama, repository of immeasurable strength, you are the son of the wind-god, born of Anjani.

3. *Mahavir Vikram Bajrangi*
   Kumati nivar sumati ke sangi

   Bravest of the braves, the great vanquisher, whose body
   is like thunder, you drive away the negative thoughts
   and bring in positive ones.

4. *Kanchan varan viraj subesa*
   Kanan kundal kunchit kesa

   Your skin glistens like gold, your clothes are pleasing.
   You have rings in your ear and your hair is curly
   and long.

5. *Hath vajra au dhvaja virajai*
   Kandhe moonj janeu sajai

   In your hands you hold a bolt of thunder and a flag.
   The sacred thread adorns your shoulder.

Hanuman at Rama's feet; calendar
art

6. *Sankar suvan Kesrinandan*
   Tej pratap maha jag vandan

   Embodiment of Shiva, scion of Kesari, your radiance is
   adored by the entire cosmos.

7. *Vidyavan guni ati chatur*
   Ram kaj karibe ko aatur

   Extremely knowledgeable, extremely clever, you are
   eager to do Rama's bidding.

8. *Prabhu charitra sunibe ko rasiya*
   Ram Lakhan Sita man basiya

   Eternally eager to hear the tales of the Lord, Rama,
   Lakshmana and Sita who eternally reside in your mind.

9. *Sukshma roop dhari Siyahi dikhava*
   Vikat roop dhari Lanka jarava

   You presented yourself before Sita in a tiny
   unthreatening form. You burnt Lanka taking a gigantic
   terrifying form.

10. *Bhima roop dhari asur sanhare*
    Ramachandra ke kaj sanvare

    In your formidable form you defeated demons and
    cheerfully performed all tasks assigned to you by Rama.

11. *Laye Sanjivan Lakhan jiyaye*
    Shri Raghuvir harashi ur laye

    You brought the magic herb that restored Lakshmana to life thus pleasing Rama.

12. *Raghupati kinhi bahut badai*
    Tum mam priy Bharatahi sam bhai

    The lord of the Raghava clan (Rama) extolled your virtues and said you were as dear to him as his brother, Bharata.

13. *Sahas badan tumharo yash gavai*
    Asa kahi Shripati kanth lagavai

    Thousands of beings will sing your praise, so saying the lord Shree (Rama) embraced you.

14. *Sankadik Brahmadi muneesa*
    Narad sarad sahit aheesa

    Sages and seers like Sanaka and Narada, Brahma (creator-god), Saraswati (goddess of learning) and Adi-Shesha (cosmic serpent) find it hard to sing your praises and extol your virtues.

Hanuman, the defender; calendar art

15. *Yam Kuber Digpal jahan te*
    Kavi kovid kahi sake kahan te

    So do the god of death (Yama), god of wealth (Kubera) and other keepers of the eight quarters. How then can a mere poet (Tulsidas) succeed in expressing your glory in verse.

16. *Tum upkar Sugreevahin keenha*
    Ram milay rajpad deenha

    You did a great service to Sugriva by uniting him with Rama and helping him gain the throne.

17. *Tumharo mantra Vibhishan mana*
    Lankeshwar bhaye sab jag jana

    By following your advice even Vibhishana, the *rakshasa*, became lord of Lanka. This the world knows.

18. *Yug sahastra yojan par Bhanu*
Leelyo tahi madhur phal janu

You traveled thousands of miles to the rising sun,
mistaking it to be a fruit.

19. *Prabhu mudrika meli mukh maheen*
Jaladhi langhi gaye achraj naheen

It is no surprise therefore that, with Rama's ring in your
mouth, you leapt across the ocean (to Lanka).

20. *Durgam kaj jagat ke jete*
Sugam anugraha tumhre tete

The burden of the world becomes light through your
grace.

Hanuman displaying Rama's image
in his heart; calendar art

21. *Ram duvare tum rakhvare,*
Hota na aagya binu paisare

You stand guard on Rama's door. No one can enter his
abode without your permission.

22. *Sab sukh lahai tumhari sarna*
Tum rakshak kahu ko darna

All comforts lie at your feet. Knowing that you are the
guardian, there is nothing to fear.

23. *Aapan tej samharo aapai*
Teenhon lok hank te kanpai

You alone can carry your dazzling glory. The three
worlds tremble at your thunderous cry.

24. *Bhoot pisach nikat nahin aavai*
Mahavir jab naam sunavai

Ghosts and vampires dare not come near when your
name is called out.

25. *Nasai rog harai sab peera*
Japat nirantar Hanumat beera

Disease, aches and pains disappear when your name is
continuously chanted.

Hanuman, the protector; calendar art

26. *Sankat te Hanuman chhudavai*
Man kram vachan dhyan jo lavai

Hanuman liberates us from all problems, when one concentrates on him, through thought, word and deed.

27. *Sab par Ram tapasvee raja*
Tin ke kaj sakal tum saja

Caretaker of Rama, you are lord and benefactor of all his devotees.

28. *Aur manorath jo koi lavai*
Sohi amit jeevan phal pavai

Whosoever thinks of you with sincerity discovers the fruit of immortal life.

29. *Charon Yug partap tumhara*
Hai parsiddh jagat ujiyara

You have been acclaimed across the entire Universe through the four ages of Time.

30. *Sadhu Sant ke tum rakhware*
Asur nikandan Ram dulare

You are the protector of sages and saints, the destroyer of demons, the beloved of Rama.

31. *Ashta siddhi nao nidhi ke data*
Asa var deen Janki mata

Bearer of the eight occult accomplishments and the nine secret treasures, you are blessed by Janaki (Sita).

32. *Ram rasayan tumhare pasa*
Sada raho Raghupati ke dasa

You hold the essence of devotion to Rama. May you remain forever the servant of the lord of the Raghava clan (Rama).

33. *Tumhare bhajan Ram ko pavai*
Janam janam ke dukh bisravai

Through your songs, Rama (Godhead) can be attained and the sorrows of several lifetimes can be forgotten.

34. *Anta kaal Raghuvarpur jayee*
Jahan janam Hari-Bhakta kahayee

Ultimately, we shall end up in Rama's divine abode where we shall reside as his devotee forever.

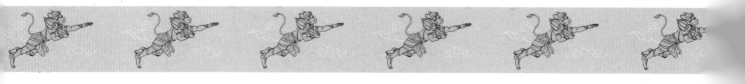

35. *Aur Devta chitta na dharaee*
    Hanumat sehi sarva sukh karaee

    There is no need to propitiate any other deity. Through
    Hanuman, all joys can be obtained.

36. *Sankat katai mitai sab peera*
    Jo sumirai Hanumat Balbeera

    All problems and pains are overcome when one
    remembers mighty Hanuman.

37. *Jai Jai Jai Hanuman Gosain*
    Kripa karahu gurudev ki nain

    Salutations Hanuman, favour me as my lord and
    master.

38. *Jo sat bar path kara koee*
    Chhutahi bandi maha sukh hoee

    Whosoever recites this Hanuman Chalisa a hundred
    times, will be liberated from the bondage of worldly life
    and attain supreme bliss.

39. *Jo yah padhai Hanuman Chalisa*
    Hoy siddhi sakhi Gaurisa

    Such is the testimony of none other than the lord of
    Gauri (Shiva).

Hanuman chanting Rama's name;
calendar art

40. *Tulsidas sada hari chera*
    Keejai Nath hriday manha dera

    Tulsidas, the eternal slave of Hari (Vishnu, Rama),
    hopes that Hanuman resides in the devotee's heart
    forever.

DOHA

    Pavan tanay sankat haran,
    Mangal murti roop.
    Ram Lakhan Sita sahit,
    Hriday basahu sur bhoop.

    Son of the wind-god, remover of all problems,
    embodiment of grace, always reside in my heart along
    with Rama, Lakshmana and Sita.

Select Bibliography

Hanuman in art, culture, thought and literature: Shanti Lal Nagar

Hanuman — art, mythology and folklore: K. C. Aryan and Subhashini Aryan

Hindu Mythology: W. J. Wilkins

Hindu World: Benjamin Walker

Many Ramayanas: Edited by Paula Richman

Puranic Encyclopaedia: Vettam Mani

Ramayana of Valmiki: translated by Makhan Lal Sen

Thai Ramayana: as written by King Rama I

Note: Stories of Hanuman are found in various tellings of the *Ramayana* such as *Valmiki Ramayana* (Sanskrit), *Adhyatma Ramayana* (Sanskrit), *Paumicariya* (Prakrit), *Rama-charitra-manas* (Hindi), *Iramavataram* (Tamil), *Molla Ramayana* (Telegu), *Bhavartha Ramayana* (Marathi), *Krittivasa Ramayana* (Bengali), *Kausika Ramayana* (Kannada), *Patala Ramayana* (Malayalam), *Madhava Kandali Ramayana* (Assamese), *Ramakirti* (Thai), *Hikayat Seri Rama* (Malay) and many more. Some stories exist only in the oral tradition.

* * *

Other Books in the Introduction Series

HINDUISM — An Introduction
Shakunthala Jagannathan

GANESHA — The Auspicious . . . The Beginning
Shakunthala Jagannathan, Nanditha Krishna

BALAJI VENKATESHWARA — An Introduction
Nanditha Krishna

SHIVA — An Introduction
Devdutt Pattanaik

VISHNU — An Introduction
Devdutt Pattanaik

DEVI, *The Mother-Goddess* — An Introduction
Devdutt Pattanaik